What people are saying
Scott Watson and Summit

"The benefits were undoubtedly gained through your amazingly magnetic and warm personality – the same materials delivered in the hands of another would not have impacted in the same way."

Recruitment and Retention Manager, Nat West Bank plc

"Scott Watson (of Summit) worked with us on a management development project in a consultancy capacity. Feedback from the individuals he worked with was very positive. He quickly gained people's trust and that resulted in them taking focused actions that benefited themselves and the business overall. He passed on tools and techniques to develop coaches and line management to achieve sustained positive behavioural change."

Head of Customer Relations, Recruitment and Training, Orange

"We received extremely positive feedback regarding the delivery of the training sessions and Summit succeeded in engaging all of the participants. Our employees and customers have seen the positive benefits of the training and I would recommend Summit to organisations that are looking for a training solution tailored to their specific needs, that engages employees and which has a tangible impact on the organisation."

Human Resources Manager, GE Capital Europe Limited

"My own, very high expectations of Summit have been exceeded and the outcomes achieved by the project team have been outstanding. Summit's approach is unique in terms of providing best advice and committing to achieving measurable improvements in performance. Personally for me, this is a refreshing change from many other training companies who shy away from remaining accountable. I recommend Summit to executives wanting to achieve outstanding results with a training company that is honest and willing to achieving real business results."

Operations Director, Sales & Direct, Bradford & Bingley plc

"Scott, thank you for a magical training event and being so very respectful to the audience."

Training Director, Roman Showers Limited

"Your bespoke approach was refreshing and it ensured that our team was left with the best possible tools to do their jobs. Following the training, an enthusiasm and commitment to success has been rekindled and they are now looking forward to the challenges their jobs may bring."

Training & Development Manager, Capita SIP Services

"The training programme was precise, tailored to our own specific needs and certainly far more effective, creative and fun than similar courses my team have undertaken in the past. The trainer made a personal connection with the team which made them feel that someone was taking a genuine interest in helping them achieve their goals rather than simply taking them through the motions of a training programme. I am personally very happy to recommend Scott Watson and Summit."

Managing Director, Frontline Display International Limited

"Scott Watson of Summit was thought provoking and dynamic in his delivery and illustrated effectively how he applies his unique personal change approaches to a wide range of human potential projects. I would certainly recommend Scott Watson to any audience wishing to laugh while they learn about how to create positive personal change with people."

Senior NCO, Her Majesty's Royal Air Force

"I am happy to recommend the services of Summit Consulting and Training Limited who have just completed a very successful training and change management project at Great Rail Journeys. Throughout the project in question the Summit team remained committed and fully involved and fulfilled a demanding brief. The project required Summit to build strong links and develop the trust of staff from all levels of the organisation and they were very successful in doing this against the backdrop of an organisation experiencing dramatic change."

Commercial Director, Great Rail Journeys Limited

"We have developed an excellent working relationship with Summit. They take great care to ensure that training is tailored to the needs of the organisation, and the courses are well researched, well prepared and delivered with energy and enthusiasm. Post-course feedback from our delegates has always been very positive."

Training and Development Manager, NUKEM Limited

WIN EVERY TIME

Essential lessons for existing and emerging leaders

Scott Watson

authorHOUSE®

AuthorHouse™
1663 Liberty Drive, Suite 200
Bloomington, IN 47403
www.authorhouse.com
Phone: 1-800-839-8640

© *2007 Scott Watson. All rights reserved.*

No part of this book may be reproduced, stored in a retrieval system, or transmitted by any means without the written permission of the author.

First published by AuthorHouse 10/31/2007

ISBN: 978-1-4259-8340-6 (sc)

Printed in the United States of America
Bloomington, Indiana

This book is printed on acid-free paper.

Many chapters have been reproduced from Croner's Personnel Management Newsletter with kind permission of Wolters Kluwer (UK) Limited (c) 2006. All rights reserved. No part of this documentation may be reproduced, stored in a retrieval system or transmitted in any form or by any means without the prior written permission of Scott Watson and Wolters Kluwer (UK) Limited. Croner is a Trading Division of Wolters Kluwer (UK) Limited.

Foreword by Professor John Thompson

It is not unusual to see management and leadership separated; but the fact remains that all managers are required to exercise leadership at certain times. Some do this well, others less well. To some managers leadership comes naturally, to others it does not.

I am not a subscriber to the argument that leadership (like entrepreneurship) can be taught – but leadership can certainly be developed to higher levels in both people for whom it comes naturally and those who have to work harder at it. This book makes a major contribution to this challenge.

Scott Watson recognises that if we are to understand how successful leaders lead effectively, we need to explore those natural behaviours that they adopt, their motivation and drive to do what they do and the techniques they utilise. The natural behaviours he discusses include kindness and keeping promises. When one thinks about this, it makes sense. People rarely (if ever!) perform at their best if they don't know what's expected of them, don't feel their efforts will be rewarded and are never taken to task in some appropriate way when their efforts fall short. And that doesn't mean they have to feel terrified. Quite the opposite, in fact. They should trust in the integrity of the person to whom they report and feel that this person in turn trusts them.

Amongst the techniques discussed are team building and appropriate training. But very significantly we also see a chapter on supplier selection and retention. Suppliers are key people upon whom organisations depend every day, sometimes to bale them out of a mess. I have often wondered how many chief executives invest as much time getting to know their major suppliers as they do talking to their major customers.

Scott Watson's new book explores the 'leadership side of management' with a comprehensive series of chapters that read like essays on key themes. His approach in each one is simple and logical – to define terms and issues, to look at the implications and why things matter, to suggest what might be done to improve performance and finally to provide questions for self-reflection.

His style is eminently readable. The material and the arguments are robust and well-researched, but easy to appreciate and easy to understand. You can be forgiven for thinking you are listening to one of his seminars as you read this book. The chapters include stories and anecdotes to give life and meaning to the arguments he is making. The text is full of insights and Watson sets out to motivate his reader to think and reflect of why the issues are important and to decide what they are going to do to improve their own performance. Watson clearly understands how managers actually learn to improve.

Each chapter can be read in around five minutes, maybe a little more in some cases – and a quick read through is a great way to start. But if you then re-read the material more slowly and reflect upon the quoted examples and factor in others from your own experiences you will begin to make more sense of the important points Watson is making. The questions at the end of each chapter can help you focus on how you might create a new personal agenda and set out to strengthen your effectiveness.

At one level this book is a very light read, but it is also a serious examination of some very important themes. It can be used flexibly and many people will benefit from exposure to the reflective thinking it encourages.

Professor John Thompson

Roger M Bale Professor of Entrepreneurship & Director of the
Business School Enterprise Network
the University of Huddersfield
United Kingdom

Introduction

Winning every time may sound like quite a challenge, even unachievable to many people in organisations. This can be especially so for those individuals who operate in leadership or management roles.

Our culture actively promotes winning in both positive and negative ways. If your organisation is bidding for a major contract or investing its marketing budget in attracting new customers, of course, you want to win and don't mind if a competitor loses. Whatever you are aiming to achieve if you seek to achieve it honestly, ethically and where everyone involved can benefit, even I will want you to win, and we haven't even met.

Leaders have so many pressing priorities such as presenting to investors, meeting with stakeholders and maintaining media relations that meeting with employees doesn't seem practical. But even when the pressures of being a corporate leader are at their highest, even if you can't be available, your trusted managers can be.

This book is not promoting you going out to win, while colleagues feel like they have lost or have had to concede their viewpoint because of your seniority rather than expertise. It is about developing leadership character where those you are paid and trusted to lead will want to follow you through genuine desire rather than obligation or necessity.

It is strange that, despite the team members at one of my clients working together for over ten years, nobody in the team knew that one man had saved the lives of two people involved in an air crash, having put aside his own safety to battle flames and drag injured passengers from the blazing aircraft. On the flip side, this is also the gentleman who stepped in some dog poo (how he knew it was a dog I am not sure) and trod it through his prospective client's office – all the way from reception, up two flights of stairs and across a crowded office of at least seventy people. It was only when his host commented on the unpleasant smell that this gentleman looked at his own shoes and noticed he was the culprit. With his colleagues and myself howling with laughter, many of us crying, this gentleman said in all seriousness, 'I know now that life deals you crap sometimes but you can always learn from it.' He didn't win the contract by the way, he did though receive a hefty carpet cleaning bill!

Acknowledgements

Thanks to Chris Shaw at Pink Elephant PR, my colleague Dirk Bansch and Craig Gordon of Gordon Publishing for their guidance and feedback during the production of this text.

To clients who demonstrate an abundance of trust and confidence towards me and my team, thank you. To my many wonderful friends who remain a constant source of encouragement and support, thank you.

Dedication

To my mum and dad Annie Elizabeth and Albert Watson for being the best parents I could ever have wished for. I continue to be inspired by your love and kindness.

xx

About the Author

Scott Watson is a highly sought after executive trainer, coach and advisor, specialising in maximising leadership, management and team effectiveness. His unique approach to personal and organisational development has made him a popular conference speaker and media commentator on the human aspects of business.

During his 12-year career with a leading UK plc, Scott realised that the quality of training and development programmes delivered by external consultancies mostly ranged from average to absolutely awful. His disappointment in dealing with fee-focused providers, delivering off-the-shelf packages that added little if any lasting value inspired him to leave the comfort of the corporate world in 1999 and launch Summit Consulting & Training. Summit has become the natural first choice for many organisations demanding results-focused, value for money training and development solutions. His motto was then and remains now "Be honest, be brilliant, be paid on time."

Under Scott's leadership, Summit has attracted clients from a wide variety of industry sectors across the globe. Clients include leading names in financial services, leisure, logistics, travel & tourism, telecommunications, utilities, healthcare, higher education, pharmaceuticals and many others; Summit continues to lead by example.

Scott's special passion is supporting humanitarian causes that help underprivileged people develop self-reliance and a more fulfilling and rewarding quality of life. A proportion of royalties from the sale of this book will be donated to a UK based charity. For details of Scott's chosen charity please visit www.WinEveryTime.co.uk

Contacting the author

For more information on corporate training, coaching and consultancy projects please explore:

www.SummitTraining.co.uk or
email **Info@SummitTraining.co.uk**

For more information on leadership and management coaching plus conference speaking events please explore:

www.ScottWatson.co.uk or email **Info@ScottWatson.co.uk**

To explore or get involved in Scott's interactive blog relating to this book please explore **www.WinEveryTime.co.uk**

Telephone +44 (0)1422 258 659

How to order more copies of this book

This book is available to organisations at a discounted price for bulk orders. Please contact the author for further information and pricing.

Contents

Chapter 1:	Trust Or Bust	1
Chapter 2:	A Promise Is A Promise	8
Chapter 3:	Attitude Is Everything... Almost!	16
Chapter 4:	Tapping Into True Potential	26
Chapter 5:	Employee Motivation – It's Easier Than You Think	36
Chapter 6:	Developing Effective Teamwork	44
Chapter 7:	Why Values-driven Organisations Stand Out From The Crowd	52
Chapter 8:	Leading By Example	61
Chapter 9:	Kindness – The Missing Piece Of The Corporate Jigsaw	70
Chapter 10:	Performance Appraisals – Necessary Evil Or Priceless Development Tool?	79
Chapter 11:	In Search Of Ethical Leadership	88
Chapter 12:	Relationships Make Things Happen	94
Chapter 13:	How To Use Training As An Employee Retention Tool	102
Chapter 14:	Before You Go And Spend A Penny...Stop!	110

How to benefit most from this book

There is no prize for finishing this book quickly. There is though a wonderful prize waiting for you if you explore the book with an open and childlike curiosity where you eagerly, even excitedly seek to learn worthwhile lessons that will serve both you and the people you are employed, paid and hopefully, trusted to lead.

When you apply the learning you will experience in this book on a day-to-day basis you will start to notice an abundance of benefits for both yourself and your team. You may be amazed with the speed that people start to communicate more openly and honestly as well as engage on a very personal level with you. In many cases this results in more efficient, productive and fulfilled teams who are prepared to go the extra mile rather than simply talk about it.

Within these pages, you will be invited to do lots of thinking. You will benefit most by reading each chapter fully. When you have read a chapter, take five or ten minutes for yourself to really think about how you can apply your learning and create some positive, worthwhile opportunities to use it with your colleagues on a day to day basis. When you have completed the book, you will benefit from revisiting the contents regularly to refresh your learning and generate some new approaches and ideas you can apply. I invite you to 'dip in' to the book randomly to review a specific chapter to support you ahead of or during a particularly challenging situation.

Other ways you can benefit from this book are to:

- ❖ Share your learning with a trusted colleague who will keep you accountable for keeping your commitment to applying the concepts you will learn.

- ❖ Work through the book with a colleague and coach each other to turn your learning in to new attitudes, habits and skills.

- ❖ Use the individual chapters as a learning opportunity for your management meeting or team away day.

CHAPTER 1:
TRUST OR BUST

The Training Director of a large Japanese conglomerate was visiting a UK plant to share his experiences on leadership and motivation and was questioned by the local management team. One executive got straight to the point: "What's the single most important factor leading to your success with staff?" he asked. The Japanese guest smiled. "We follow the four T's", he said. His audience were very experienced senior people but this was a new concept to them. They asked for further guidance.

"First", said the guest "we train them. Next we train them. Then we train them again." "And then what happens?" asked the audience. "Ah", said the guest, "Then we trust them! We trust them to do their work, to report problems, to raise concerns, to share successes, to make jobs easier and to contribute to the success of our enterprise. We also conduct our affairs as managers in a style that encourages our staff to trust us. This is also of vital importance if we are to succeed."

Trust is earned and is a two-way street

Following the final T is something that can be easily forgotten in organisations, whatever their size or sector. To use the old adage, trust is earned and is a two-way street. Trust is built by all concerned speaking and acting truthfully and with commitment at all times, even when unpleasant matters need to be debated and resolved.

One dictionary definition of trust reads as follows: - *reliance on the integrity, strength, ability and surety of a person or thing; confidence.*

Democritus summed it up succinctly as long ago as 400BC when he said "Do not trust all men, but trust men of worth; the former course is silly, the latter a mark of prudence."

Trust is clearly crucial in the overall successful operation of any organisation; a fact that has been recognised yet frequently ignored for over two thousand years. The absence of trust drags down performance and is perhaps the single main contributory factor in teams failing to engage with their managers or achieve their goals. Just as importantly, it prevents the establishment of optimum and harmonious working relationships that are so vital to success in any enterprise.

Trust takes years to develop and seconds to destroy

It may be an old saying, but it remains true nevertheless. Think back just a few years to the Enron, WorldCom and Parmalat cases. Do you think that their customers still view them in quite the same light as they did before these scandals? If they do, they may be forgiven for being somewhat naive. These organisations may, at the time of writing, have managed to survive in some form, despite the adverse media and regulatory attention they received, but what message has been transmitted to their remaining employees? At very best, those still working will be conscious of a feeling of acute distrust in the most senior people and it may take a very long time to reverse this perception.

A high level of trust between colleagues demonstrates that people believe in and respect each other

On the other side of the coin, when high levels of trust exist between leaders, managers and front-line employees, it enables ordinary people to achieve extraordinary things. When partnered by technical competence, high levels of trust encourage employees at all levels not only to want to contribute more but to be involved in making their own unique contribution to the success of their organisation. They will be more motivated to develop genuine win-win relationships, where hidden agendas and back-biting are a rare occurrence. In the event of either of these latter situations arising, in most cases they tend to be dealt with privately, quickly, effectively and, perhaps surprisingly, amicably.

As Thomas Moore once said, "We need people in our lives with whom we can be as open as possible. To have real conversations with people may seem like such a simple, obvious suggestion, but it involves courage and risk."

A high level of trust between colleagues demonstrates that people believe in and respect each other. It encourages everyone in the organisation to be more open with and supportive of one another. This helps ideas to flow, problems to be solved more quickly and performance to be improved, sometimes beyond a level anyone could have possibly expected. The status of the leader is also reinforced by him or her becoming genuinely more approachable and demonstrating a desire to support and further develop the trusting nature of their teams while, of course, ensuring that the required levels of performance are being achieved or indeed exceeded.

On an organisational level, when trust is broken, investors may walk away taking trusting customers with them in the process. The same applies for employees who feel they have been managed in a similar manner, intentionally or otherwise. The end result is that an absence of trust leads to experience, knowledge, flair and ability haemorrhaging away with some of the people lost to one organisation invariably gravitating to the competition where their talents can, and probably will, be exploited willingly and with ruthless efficiency.

When trust is absent – how bad can it become?

Think back to an example of what happens when trust has deteriorated, and recall the experience of British Airways (BA) in 2004. The problems here were profound, with staff effectively demonstrating their feelings of lack of engagement with the company by declining to attend work for the most minor medical reasons. Absenteeism had risen to the point where the typical BA employee was taking seventeen days annual 'sick' leave, an unacceptable level to BA's top executives and indicative of the general lack of engagement between employer and employees.

BA attempted to resolve this issue by concluding a pay negotiation that included paying staff more for taking less 'sick' days, a strange manoeuvre when it was acknowledged that inadequate communication and a breakdown of trust, not inadequate salaries and benefits, had created the circumstances they were experiencing. What was really needed was the start of some serious bridge-building to ensure that everyone in the enterprise genuinely believed that they were an important and valued part of what, according to the marketing bosses at BA, was, "the world's favourite airline", and that their involvement actually mattered.

How can trust be improved within organisations?

The initiative to improve trust must start at the very top. Every person in a position of responsibility must, as well as being technically competent in their role, authentically and consistently impart their message truthfully, accurately and even passionately. Keeping quiet about problems and difficulties as well as successes is simply not an option. As Martin Luther King Jnr once remarked, "Our lives begin to end the day we become silent about things that matter."

This statement is just as valid in the corporate arena as it is with regard to civil rights. Promises and commitments made must be upheld, because this is how trust is demonstrated, nurtured and maintained.

The best way to develop trust is to be trustworthy; worthy of being trusted

The best way to develop trust is to be trustworthy; worthy of being trusted. Just think about it. Wouldn't it be appreciated if your staff were asked for their input on an issue where they had something to contribute? Wouldn't they rather be praised or even reprimanded by a manager they trusted? In the former case they would appreciate the recognition being shown while in the latter they would understand that they weren't being punished, simply being reminded of how things should be done and what was expected of them. Individuals, teams and organisations react to enhanced trust very positively, and those organisations where it is genuinely a two-way event are invariably those where success is the norm, not the exception.

Establishing a culture of trust within the working environment can yield incredibly positive results in the same manner that failing to do so can tilt the pendulum the other way just as effectively. The proof? I have personally interviewed over one-hundred managers who chose to resign from their organisation. Most cited a lack of trust and belief in their directors or senior managers as the single most common cause of their departure. Could it be that the experience of more junior personnel would be broadly similar?

Only by taking a long hard look at their organisation, can leaders truly determine what levels of trust exist within it. Where problems are apparent, a leader needs to react to ensure that their organisation becomes one not just based on trust, but where trusting each other becomes a way of life. Like anything else in life, it does become easier with practice. Trust me!

Something to think about...

- ✓ What would you do when asked to brief your team with a message that you knew to be not altogether truthful?

- ✓ How would you react to a colleague who you knew was frequently untrustworthy?

- ✓ What could you do starting right now to develop more trust within your team and also with your superiors?

- ✓ What do you feel you have to do to ensure that you could always trust your team?

- ✓ What do you feel you have to do to ensure that your team know that they could always trust you?

My Notes

CHAPTER 2:
A PROMISE IS A PROMISE

What happens when politicians make a promise – even if they don't use the word – and then don't keep it? A prime example is that of George Bush Snr, when he accepted the Republican Party nomination to run for President of the United States of America in 1988.

"Read My Lips, No New Taxes," is the statement made by Bush Snr that is still remembered two decades later, and which resulted in a long-standing loss of credibility for the presidential candidate.

When a promise or commitment is made, isn't it fair and reasonable that an individual should reserve the right to change their mind? Perhaps they made the promise to appease an overbearing boss. Or maybe they were so committed to their team or organisation that they wanted to make a very personal contribution for the right reasons, but then realised that it would be impossible to keep due to conflicting priorities and tight deadlines.

But when a person continually makes and then breaks promises, it could be valuable to speak privately with them in order to understand exactly why this pattern repeatedly occurs. This type of conversation relies heavily on open, honest dialogue and trust and must be undertaken with a win-win outcome very much in mind.

Most leaders I have met would much rather a colleague tell them "No I can't achieve that deadline due to other pressing priorities you have asked me to deliver" rather than a blanket "Yes, of course I'll do it right now" which is not only submissive but ultimately can damage the effectiveness of the team or organisation.

One method that works wonderfully well is when a leader briefs a team member in fine detail, helping them understand the goal to be achieved, resources available, potential pitfalls and benefits of achieving a positive outcome. When a person understands this information in detail – and is also supported throughout the process – they are far more likely to be successful in delivering the desired outcomes.

Deliver what you promise

Stephen Hemsley, CEO of Domino's Pizza in the UK and Ireland, is quoted as saying: "The underlying business strategy is to deliver what you promise… Our credibility would have been blown if we had gone out with extensive television advertising and the experience that the customer enjoyed did not meet or exceed what we promised." The most recent figures show that Domino's Pizza has over 7500 stores in over 50 countries.

Mr Hemsley also points out that effective communication is a vital ingredient to maximise the success of his enterprise – it is the relationship developed with franchisees that supports the delivery of Domino's promise to its customers. After all, their promise is to deliver fresh baked pizza within 30 minutes of the customer order being received. Quite a challenge, but they consistently deliver on their promise and this has in no small way supported their profitable and rapid expansion.

Why are promises important?

One dictionary defines a 'promise' as *"a declaration assuring that one will or will not do something, a vow."* What might happen if your closest friend made promises to you but never kept them? Would his or her action, or lack of it, help your friendship flourish or would it serve to destroy trust and respect?

If the latter is your likely response, relate this decision to your employees that took so long to recruit and your customers who took what felt like forever to acquire and can prove even more difficult to retain with increased competition in the marketplace.

What judgments might your employees and customers be making that will negatively impact on your relationship with them? When people feel let down, they rarely say anything, choosing to keep quiet rather than discuss the problem, as they don't want to make the situation worse. This in itself serves to make the situation worse as open, honest dialogue ceases to exist.

Isn't it strange that in business many people don't only want you to commit to doing (or not doing) something? They feel the need to upgrade your "Yes, I'll do that by the deadline set" with a doubting look followed by the question "You promise?" It's almost as if the word promise not only makes your commitment more solid in their own mind but, if you fail to achieve the deadline agreed, it is also far easier for the other person to absolve themselves of any shared responsibility for the failure by simply telling their boss or customer "Well, she promised it would be done and I took her word for it."

But when someone asks you to make a promise, what underlying message are they communicating? Is it that they trust you implicitly to do your best in a spirit of genuine teamwork and partnership? Or could it be more likely that he or she lacks confidence that you will keep your commitment, and wants some form of additional reassurance for his or her own peace of mind? It could be worth remembering that people judge us on whether we actually deliver on our undertakings to them, whether the word used is 'commitment' or 'promise'.

"Here's a list of promises we think we might be able to keep."

The empty price promise

Recently, I decided to buy a new digital camera and in my home town noticed a large sign displayed in the window of a well-known photographic store that read "Find the same deal cheaper anywhere else and we promise to match or beat the competitor's price." Great news, or so I thought. It was only upon my presenting the price to be matched to the store manager from an internet retailer that I became aware of the empty price promise. The internet retailer's price was nearly £100 cheaper.

Upon reading the internet quote, the store manager said in a nervous, almost apologetic tone "Erm, the erm thing is that our price promise doesn't include prices from the Internet. It only applies to quotes from other camera shops in the town." The fact is that the sign emblazoned over the store front did not mention such a condition and there is only one other camera store in my home town, less than 50 yards from this store! Perhaps a more accurate sign would have read "Find the same deal cheaper anywhere else (within 50 yards of our store) and we promise to match or beat the competitor's price."

When promises go unfulfilled, employees become cynical and customers leave to find an alternative provider

It is possible that the store manager had the 'price promise' imposed on him by his head office but may not have realised the impact of the misleading marketing, and how it can destroy trust and profitability in seconds. The quickest, most effective way for any organisation in any industry to lose credibility and destroy trust with both employees and customers is to make a promise and then break it. Whether it is a recruitment advertisement promising 'ongoing development opportunities' that never materialise, or a price promise that is misleading or even dishonest, if the promise isn't upheld, it won't work. People are becoming more savvy and will be insulted and alienated by the action.

A common practice in organisations is for employees at all levels to commit to achieving specific outcomes or meeting tough deadlines, knowing in advance they cannot possibly meet such expectations – and therefore living to regret committing themselves. Promises are often made to appease a demanding boss or challenging customer. But what is often overlooked in these instances is that such submissive behaviour could ultimately cause the person to lose his or her job due to performing below agreed standards; and the organisation to lose customers and credibility as trust and patience vanish. Ultimately, when promises go unfulfilled, colleagues, customers and suppliers become cynical and untrusting, always being extra cautious when planning future dealings. To develop credibility, trust and great relationships, it is vital that promises made are kept as long as they are designed to benefit all parties.

If you feel you will not be able to keep a promise, simply do not make it in the first place. Or, if a situation arises outside of your control that delays progress, at least have a relationship with your stakeholders where the problem is acknowledged and moved towards a solution with everybody's integrity intact and contingency plans implemented.

Something to think about...

The key factors involved in keeping corporate promises are:

- ✓ Don't under promise and over deliver as it lacks integrity. Just say what you will do and then do it.

- ✓ Develop relationships based on integrity as well as technical capability.

- ✓ Live your personal values more often. Even during a disagreement people appreciate authenticity.

- ✓ Open, honest communication is vital to maximising success. Start with the end in mind and nurture the relationship so it can flourish for everyone's benefit.

- ✓ Remember that it adds no value to agree to an unachievable deadline. When telling the other party it can't be achieved, remember to give them a suitable alternative as to what can be achieved without sacrificing the quality of outputs.

- ✓ Always be honest – not only will it develop deep levels of rapport, trust and credibility, it is also much easier to remember.

- ✓ Plan your priorities precisely and build in adequate time to ensure that both quality and speed of outputs are achievable without panic.

WIN EVERY TIME

My Notes

CHAPTER 3:
ATTITUDE IS EVERYTHING... ALMOST!

As the old saying goes, we get what we focus our minds on. If we think we are going to be stressed during a presentation or fail miserably at delivering an important project, you can guess what will happen. We will certainly be stressed and we will fail miserably. Every leader has either witnessed or experienced this draining approach to thinking during is or her career. Indeed one of the most common people issues that a human resources team has to deal with is what is commonly termed a 'bad attitude'.

***If your organisation has two thousand employees,
It has the same number of attitudes***

Attitude is such a complex subject. One dictionary defines attitude as "*a state of mind or a feeling.*" Might it therefore be more useful to take responsibility for our attitudes and accept that they are merely a personal choice? If your organisation has two thousand employees, it has the same number of attitudes, right? If this is starting to sound a little scary, it should, because ultimately it is the responsibility of the leadership team to recruit, retain and develop employees with a good attitude towards their work and colleagues. The level of success an organisation achieves is largely a direct reflection of the mental focus and attitude of its employees.

The role of attitude on our working lives

If employees have an absolute belief in their employer, the goods or services it provides and their own personal ability to make a meaningful contribution in their role, they are likely to succeed and add value to the organisation.

Think about it for a moment. In your workplace, do you notice that some people are just so positive, excited and energetic throughout the week? They seem to deal with any challenge that comes their way in a positive manner and resolve matters quickly with little fuss. Nothing seems to get them down; even during the tough times they remain positive. On the other hand, there may also be some colleagues who have less serious challenges but deal with them in such a negative manner that they behave as though their world is falling apart and there is nothing they can do to stop it happening – they turn themselves into helpless victims who see themselves as being at the mercy of their circumstances, at least in their own mind. They can become angry, frustrated, and complain that everyone and everything is against them, blaming others for their situation and how they feel (*Of course, I'm not for a moment implying that you might do that sometimes*).

This kind of thinking and subsequent external behaviour can help to abdicate responsibility for the delivery of the commitments previously made, with deadlines being missed, relationships damaged and trust disappearing. Ultimately, the organisation suffers.

A Case Study

A good example of how attitude can affect performance can be seen in the following case study. A head teacher told a class of young school children that their intelligence was dictated purely by their eye colour. Blue-eyed children were said to be far more intelligent than children with eyes of other colours, therefore blue-eyed kids were superior and the other kids were inferior.

The class was separated into two groups. The blue-eyed children in one room with one teacher and the non-blue eyed children with another teacher. The blue-eyed children flourished, with test scores and speed of learning surpassing even the teacher's expectations while the performance of the other class fell through the floor. Many children actually performed worse than they did before the head teacher's comments. They were falling apart. Could it be that the second group were living down to the low expectations set in the same manner that the first group were living up to the high expectations set for them?

Two weeks into the experiment, the head teacher brought the two teachers together and said that she had got it wrong. It was really the blue-eyed children who were inferior and not the other group. The teachers were instructed to return to their classes, inform their pupils of her error and continue teaching. The blue-eyed children's results deteriorated almost immediately, with more wrong answers to 'easy' questions, creativity disappearning and unacceptable behaviour became more common in class. The non-blue-eyed children suddenly started to enjoy learning more, and the improvement in results shocked both the teacher and the children. As if by magic they became more creative and well behaved.

So why did this change in performance happen? The attitude of the head teacher rubbed off on her teachers, the teachers' attitudes rubbed off on their pupils. Following the experiment the children were told about it and no lasting harm was done. It is exactly the same principle that applies in the workplace.

Can't do v Can do

A negative attitude serves to focus attention on limitations and barriers, many of which don't actually exist in the external world, only being figments of our imagination. This approach can also place responsibility for how we feel and perform on someone other than ourselves and this mindset can easily degenerate into a blame driven attitude.

We human beings can be really good at making excuses in advance of a situation arising, mentally rehearsing them for later when we tell people that we have failed yet again. Before attending a job interview it could be "I probably won't get the job anyway," or when the need to address a performance issue with a colleague arises it may be "They will go crazy and it will turn into an argument so I had better not mention the problem." The outcomes of these situations are dependent on someone else's interpretation of our communication and that is why we could all benefit from learning to focus more on how to generate the best possible outcome, whatever the situation may be.

To demonstrate how powerful attitude can be, consider the achievements of athlete, Sir Roger Bannister and his record breaking success. He was the first human being to be officially recorded as running a sub four-minute mile and was hailed as being 'superhuman'. Yet, within several years of him breaking the four-minute mile barrier, many other athletes were recorded as running one mile in less than four minutes. But how could this happen? Of course, there are many factors to be considered, but it was due largely to the fact that other athletes' attitudes changed because they had evidence that it could be achieved.

One of the most powerful comments I have heard in quite while came from Henry Ford who said, "If you think you can or you think you can't, you're right." That statement encapsulated the effect of attitude better than any textbook on the subject of attitude and is a phrase worth remembering.

Scott Watson

Attitudes are contagious

It is essential that the leadership team demonstrates positive, can do, supportive and optimistic attitudes on a daily basis

How do you think your attitude rubs off on your colleagues and customers? Remember that employees will copy the attitudes displayed by their leaders and senior managers. It is therefore essential that the leadership team demonstrates positive, 'can do', supportive and optimistic attitudes on a daily basis if corporate effectiveness is to be maximised and talent retained long-term.

It is dangerous though to allow a positive mind set to mask incompetence or lack of expertise. It is a positive attitude coupled with technical competence working together that achieves extraordinary results. Perhaps the greatest recent exponent of this was heavyweight boxing champion Muhammad Ali, who mesmerised the sporting world by reciting poetry about forthcoming fights and how he would exploit the inadequacies of his opponents. He was also not exactly bashful at advising the world that he was indeed, 'The Greatest'. Love him or loathe him, he backed up the rhetoric with some of the most stunning boxing performances ever witnessed. He truly did possess the skills, talent, ability AND positive attitude to make things happen and reserve his place in the history books. Just as importantly, Ali often spoke about unity and friendship, bringing opposing sides together and developing a shared understanding and appreciation of individuals to create a better world. Such qualities are a reflection of true leadership in action.

Other well known figures from recent history have also commented meaningfully on attitude, occasionally in the most thought provoking ways. It was Mother Teresa of Calcutta who said, "In this life we cannot do great things. We can only do small things with great love." She knew that she didn't have a magic wand that would allow her to eradicate the ills of the poor people surrounding her, but she did possess an attitude that drove her to do all she could to help them. Think also about a very wry comment made by civil rights leader, the late Martin Luther King Jnr when he said, "It may be true that the law cannot make a man love me, but it can keep him from lynching me, and I think that's pretty important." It is certainly a different way to approach 'attitude' but it was undoubtedly an observation that demonstrated how to turn a 'negative' into a 'positive'.

Attitude on a personal level

Attitude isn't something that must only happen in the workplace. Having a positive attitude to life in general will also reap rich rewards. Don't believe it? Well, hundreds of health studies around the globe have shown that a positive, optimistic attitude contributes to a happier and more fulfilling quality of life, whereas a negative attitude can lead to mental and emotional challenges such as depression, anxiety and manifest related problems in later life. The evidence is clear; if you and your colleagues want to experience more enjoyment and fulfilment in everything that you do, adopt a positive attitude to life and the world in general. The fact that such an approach will provide more happiness, stability, success and a feeling of general well-being can't be a bad thing, can it?

If you still aren't convinced, here is another example of a medical case study, something involving life and death, and it doesn't get more personal than that. The following phenomenon is called the placebo effect – There are hundreds of case studies where hospital patients have been prescribed 'medication' that was simply nothing more than sugar pills but they were convinced by their doctor that the medication was a cure for their condition or at the very least, would result in a speedy improvement in their state of health and well-being. Amazingly, the health of many patients suddenly improved – simply because they viewed their situation differently and subsequently, their attitude changed, no other reason.

Your attitude is your choice and responsibility

Time now to consider what you are going to do to ensure that you consistently and truthfully present a positive attitude about yourself and people you lead and work with. Remember, every morning when you wake up, you have the choice to face the day with a positive or negative attitude. It is as simple as that and only you can make the decision. Having a positive attitude all day every day is quite a challenge, perhaps unrealistic. After all, if we didn't experience the occasional low point, we wouldn't be able to appreciate the highs. The skill is to acknowledge when we are entering a position of negative attitude and then decide to change your mental focus to move you out of it as quickly and easily as possible.

Making the right decision each day and demonstrating a positive attitude, even about the challenges that crop up with frustrating regularity will help you to be recognised as a person showing confidence in the future. And such people do get noticed: by their superiors as well as their peers and the workforce reporting to them. You owe it to yourself to cultivate a positive attitude; especially when the going gets tough and others around you are despondent. So how can you do it?

Perhaps one idea is to remember that you can't change the past, you can only influence the future; but you can control how you think and how you feel in the present moment. Putting this another way, when last months sales figures look appalling, or a colleague lets you down, or the deal you hoped to clinch turned sour, remember it's history. Those people with a negative attitude are likely to spend the whole day or even longer bemoaning their fate, while the positive thinkers will take a deep breath and reflect on the fact that what has gone has gone, lessons have been learned, and that things can and will be done better next time around. Think about it; which category would you rather your manager be in? Start adopting a positive attitude, even in times of adversity, and those around you will soon start to recognise that you are the person they want to be associated with. Such people invariably flourish, independent of the position they hold and the role they undertake.

Something to think about...

- ✓ Remember that you can't change the past, but you can certainly learn from it.

- ✓ No matter what the circumstances, endeavour to explore how a benefit might arise from any adverse situation.

- ✓ Encourage those around you to think positively as attitudes are contagious.

- ✓ Continue learning and sharpening the skills needed to enable you to do your job – and the next one up the ladder – even better. Skills + attitude are a potent combination.

- ✓ If you think you can or think you can't, you're right!

WIN EVERY TIME

My Notes

CHAPTER 4:
TAPPING INTO TRUE POTENTIAL

The scorching hot summer months had attracted an abundance of customers for the steamboat owner and he was rubbing his hands in anticipation of yet another bumper day on the river. Business had never been so good. So it was a rather unwelcome shock when he opened the valves to start the engine to hear nothing more than a splutter. Time after time he continued to adjust the settings, each time with more and more anxiety. "This just can't be happening to me, not today of all days," he muttered to himself.

But it was happening, and he needed to get the engine fixed, and fast. The boat's owner tried one expert after another, but none of them could figure out how to fix the engine. He was running out of options so in a final desperate attempt to get his boat working, he called in an old man who had been fixing boats since he was a youngster.

The old man arrived wearing a rather tattered and torn blue boiler suit and carrying a small tool bag. He immediately headed toward the engine room and set to work. He inspected the engine very carefully, top to bottom. The boat's owner was there, watching with hope that this man would know what to do. After inspecting the vast maze of pipes, the old man casually reached into his bag and pulled out a small hammer. He gently tapped one of the pipes and instantly, the engine sprang to life. The engine was fixed, his job was done and the steamboat owner breathed a sigh of relief.

A week later, the boat owner received a bill from the old man for one thousand pounds. "This is daylight robbery!" he shouted when reading the bill. "He hardly did anything!" He telephoned the old man and insisted that an itemised bill be produced and sent to him before payment of this outrageous bill would be considered further.

The old man sent a bill that simply read:

For 15 minutes of tapping	£2
For knowing where to tap	£998
Total	£1000

Knowledge and Power

The bill was paid and the steam boat owner was no doubt left to reflect on the fact that knowledge is indeed power. It is also one of the few things that can be given away freely, yet retained entirely by the owner; but that's another story in itself.

The same principle applies to leading and working within teams. Knowing how to tap into the skills, knowledge and experience of individuals within the team is something that the leader ignores at his or her peril. Yet it happens all the time, and is arguably one of the greatest hidden losses experienced within the UK working environment. Knowledge certainly isn't power if it is allowed to lie dormant and when it is hidden so close to hand it's positively folly. And yet...

Personal Impact

Like it or not, we all have an impact on other people, whether positive or negative, and it is worth remembering that people make their minds up about us almost instantly. First impressions are, therefore, important. What we do from there on though becomes even more vital.

Think for a moment about some of history's remembered people. Martin Luther King Jnr, Gandhi, Mother Teresa of Calcutta, Winston Churchill to name but a few. Each had a very different style of communicating with people, but they all had one thing in common – they created deep and meaningful connections with other human beings in different ways, at different times, and in different circumstances for different reasons.

Time now to do some thinking that could feel a little uncomfortable, so take a few deep breaths and examine your personal impact.

What impact do you create with the people you are trusted to lead and work alongside? Do you create a negative environment where hidden agendas, poor quality relationships and suspicion abound, or do you nurture positive relationships and underpin your daily actions and activities with strong personal values and standards that are understood and respected? Be honest with yourself and perhaps also invite one or two trusted colleagues to provide you with some candid feedback that will enhance your self-awareness in this area and support you in becoming an even more effective leader.

If you wish to be a leader of others and a successful one at that, you need to do everything in your power to place yourself in the latter category. Sure, you can probably survive in the former, but invariably not for long and you won't feel at all comfortable while you are there. There is little point in holding a leadership position if, when you look over your shoulder, you find that nobody in your team is following you. And that is what can happen if employees are actively disengaged from their work and their relationships. This directly impacts the quality of outputs achieved.

As mentioned above, different times and circumstances demand different approaches. For example, you would hardly expect to lead a company of commandos into battle using the same motivational techniques as those deployed with a group of supermarket check-out operators. Paradoxically, the key to success in both instances however, remains the same, although you would use very different routes to arrive at the same end point.

The secret is that you need to create an environment in which people will follow you through desire, not obligation. The good news is that while there will always be 'born-leaders' whose natural charm and charisma attracts others to work for them and go the extra mile all the time, the necessary techniques can be learned and successfully deployed by lesser mortals like you and I. One of the truly frightening things is that few leaders or managers invest any time and energy to find out what these techniques are and remain cocooned in their own sphere of influence, blind to the opportunities that lie waiting.

What has happened to you?

A leader is a person you will follow to a place you wouldn't go by yourself
Joel Arthur Barker

I would venture to suggest that if you take a moment to reflect on your own personal career you will remember people who inspired you. The people who worked hard themselves and gave you credit when you contributed to the overall effort; the people with a positive, enthusiastic, 'can do' approach, those who weren't frightened to say "I really need your help with this project," and those who seemed to have an incredible grasp of what needed doing to achieve the desired results, no matter what the problem. As Joel Arthur Barker, the first person to popularise the concept of paradigm shifts for the corporate world, once said, "A leader is a person you will follow to a place you wouldn't go by yourself."

Regrettably, it is perhaps even more likely that you will also have encountered others who failed completely to inspire. I'm sure you know the type; those who drifted into work and left when it suited them, yet criticised you openly the first time you were five minutes late back from lunch. The aggressive bully who shouted at everyone in the belief that if the team was frightened it would perform more effectively. The one who imagined he or she had all the answers yet in reality knew very little, and the person who had been elevated to a position of trust and management and was clearly out of their depth. Ask yourself the question, "What did I dislike most about them?" and then ask the much more difficult question, "Am I guilty of some of the same sins?" When we realise and admit to ourselves that we occasionally treat people unfairly or even unkindly, albeit unwittingly, we can then go about rectifying the situation in a positive manner.

Welcome to the Goldmine

Jumping back a little now, what are these techniques that we can all learn to help us become better leaders and managers of others?

Remember, the key is to create a genuine desire in others to achieve a task or solve an identified problem, and as you might expect from what has been noted previously, there are many ways to accomplish this depending on the people themselves and the circumstances which prevail at a particular time. Independent of the circumstances, however, experience confirms that people from a very wide cross-section of society perform best when four clearly defined criteria are observed.

They understand the 'Challenge'

The use of inverts here is very deliberate because 'challenge' covers almost everything that a team or individual might be called upon to do. It can mean "How can we increase our margins by 5% within six months?" It can mean "Where can we source XYZ in accordance with main board directives on environmental considerations, or how do we eliminate queues at the basket-only checkouts?" Only if the team and individuals understand exactly what results are needed can they set about their work in a structured fashion focused on problem solving.

They are involved in the decision making process

Good leaders will call their teams together, explain the challenge, and then review with everyone ways and means to achieve the desired results. At this point the good leader will invariably be able to lead because he or she will have been aware of the challenge for some time before the rest of the team and will, if they are worth their salt, have been thinking about potential solutions for some time.

The fact that you are exploring options with your team is a powerful motivator and demonstrates your respect for them and their ideas. It also shows that you are not afraid to share knowledge and that you are willing to support ideas that flow from subordinates. Keep in mind that your job is to lead, not to DO everything. Do not lose sight of the fact, however, that at the end of this process, YOU are the one who has to make the final decision and take responsibility for the outcome. Whatever you do decide, however, will invariably have the support of your team, and that's a fantastic start to any venture.

Advertise the project, set milestones, and monitor progress

Once the desired and agreed outcomes have been identified, it is essential that you issue a programme confirming where responsibilities lie and the timescales involved. Only by doing this can everyone including you be 100% aware of their responsibilities. And, if you have misinterpreted anything that was agreed, you can be sure people will let you know.

Monitoring progress against targets is crucially important and here the good leader will be able to demonstrate his or her skills by interpreting events and initiating any changes necessary. This sometimes means taking very difficult decisions because as you have sown, so will you have to reap. If someone is genuinely struggling to achieve a result, it is your duty to support them wherever and whenever possible, and get other team members on board with their support as well. If, at the end of the day, however, they can't perform to the required standard, then re-deployment in some form may need to be initiated. The same approach will also be necessary with those who won't perform, although their re-deployment should occur somewhat swifter as they will be dragging down the efforts of the rest of the team. As the leader, you will gain the respect of the team by dealing with such an issue sympathetically, dispassionately and quickly.

Share the success

This means exactly what it says. Because most projects will be entered into with no guarantee of success, even if you don't achieve the desired objective, providing you and your team have given it your very best shot then you will have learned a great deal and proved that the result cannot be obtained using the methodology and techniques you elected to deploy. This in turn means that the next time the challenge or problem is addressed; you know which avenues not to pursue. There really is no such thing as failure under these circumstances, just a realisation of the need to explore different approaches and remain solution-focused.

Don't believe me? Well it took the human race about 15 million years to learn to fly and only by trying different things did we succeed.

At the end of a project, share the outcome and successes with the team, thank them for their efforts and let them know you genuinely appreciate all their endeavours. If you do this you can bet that they will be rubbing their hands at the thought of the next project working for and with you.

What Now?

What have you done over the last few months that qualifies you as a leader? What is the situation that you are really proud of? Have you really earned your salary as a leader, or have you been content to let things merely take their course?

Frightening questions aren't they, and ones that the good leader will be addressing several times each month as he or she strives to maintain the focus on doing what is right for the long-term health and success of the organisation, the team and individuals. The good leader will also be constantly observing his or her people and seeking ways to tap into their skills, knowledge and experience and bringing them to bear on the day-to-day issues which can contribute so effectively to the efficient running of any organisation, be it small or multi-national. This means knowing your people and knowing them well.

Given that we human beings are incredibly complex entities who are affected by a myriad of ever-changing factors, this is one of the hardest things to achieve and you will never get it right all the time. A great leader who knows his or her people, however, will have a high success rate and be able to adjust their approach to appeal to the circumstances prevailing at different times and against different backgrounds.

Accept right now that it isn't easy, and that you will sometimes fail. This all constitutes part of the risk/reward ratio that makes leadership such a fascinating and rewarding subject. Only the dedicated will succeed and it is they who will experience the warm glow of inner satisfaction that comes of knowing their chosen field so well. It is these people who invariably become so sought after by other employers and go on to accomplish great things. This may be a long way removed from knowing where to hit a pipe with a hammer, but the connection remains valid.

Scott Watson

One story on the subject of knowing your team and getting the best from them arose during the dark days of World War Two. A famous General was asked by his junior officers what made him the man the ordinary soldiers would literally follow through mud and bullets. He replied by removing a shoelace and laying it in the desk pointing towards the questioner. "Push that back to me," he said, "but make sure it stays straight."

Of course, when pushed, the shoelace twisted all over the place and the junior officer no doubt felt a little perplexed. The General then placed his finger on the end nearest him and dragged the shoelace in a perfectly straight line back towards himself. "Leadership is about leading, not about pushing," said the General. Today's great leaders understand this, and know it to be as true today as it was then.

In conclusion then, if you have people working for you, you have your very own goldmine probably sat at the very next desk and certainly within reach of a phone call, even if your colleagues work on the other side of the globe. If you want to start picking up a few nuggets, perhaps you ought to talk.

My Notes

CHAPTER 5:
EMPLOYEE MOTIVATION – IT'S EASIER THAN YOU THINK

Much has been written about the need for and value of motivation in the workplace. However, developing and maintaining high levels of motivation remains a challenge for many organisations. There are several key qualities and behaviours that underpin the development and maintenance of high levels of motivation and these are:

Setting a clear context for employees

A crucial factor that leaders need to be aware of is the value of setting a clear context for employees from the outset. If employees have a clear understanding of their role, their responsibilities and the value that their contribution adds to the organisation, they will usually want to perform well. If they feel that their role is both challenging and fulfilling, their positive attitude will not only be noticed by colleagues and customers, but will subtly manifest a similar attitude in return. When individuals develop a meaningful relationship with their work and their leaders they are more likely to perform well, even through the most challenging of times.

Credible, supportive leadership

Credible, supportive leadership is vital to maximising employee motivation. This type of leadership is not based purely on technical expertise; while this is an essential ingredient, the value of personal qualities such as trust, respect, integrity and honesty cannot be overstated.
The absence of such qualities in leadership teams leads almost automatically to low levels of motivation, inferior performance and a gradual dilution of employee loyalty. But credible, supportive leadership does not mean that employees have free reign to do as they wish. In this relationship, everybody is clear on their role, responsibilities and also what is expected of them in terms of their conduct and communication with others in the workplace.

Authentic communication is vital

Motivation levels are almost always high when employees feel that their relationship with their manager is open, honest and mutually supportive.

Few things destroy working relationships faster than an absence of trust or the pursuit of personal agendas based more on ego and a need to feel significant at the expense of others. When authentic communication is the norm, each person has express permission to speak up when they feel they should challenge procedures and policies if they feel it adds value and, ultimately, feel empowered to make their own unique contribution to their team and organisation overall. In this type of relationship mutual trust, respect and support abound and an individual's right to be heard is both understood and welcomed. Remember, trust can take months to develop, but can be lost in just a few seconds.

Please, please, please stop building rafts

Well-meaning leaders sometimes choose a team-building event as a means to enhance employee motivation. While their intention is overwhelmingly positive and commendable, such events do very little to support enhanced motivation and improved performance back in the real world of work.

Team-building events do have their place, but please get them in context. They can help teams to improve relationships, communication and focus, but building rafts or abseiling are not a replacement for credible leadership and management. It is a brave, or perhaps foolish, leader who believes a day out in the countryside with a free bar in the evening will make recurring problems disappear or help achieve exemplary performance.

Doing the right thing

High levels of motivation promote high levels of effectiveness and performance, while low levels of motivation produce the exact opposite. What's more, we all know how difficult it can be to snap out of such an emotional state, even if it is only having to undertake a household chore such as washing the dishes – never mind leading or working within a team where excellence is expected or demanded.

When I speak about 'catching people doing things right' members of the audience will often quickly challenge my comment – as if praising someone for exceeding expectations, resolving a complex problem or dealing effectively with a customer complaint will be perceived as 'touchy-feely' and unwelcome. Of course, the exact opposite is true; when someone receives genuine praise for doing a great job, good relationships withstanding, they will almost always accept a 'well done' or 'thank you' – if their relationship with the messenger is productive and trusting.

Naturally, I am not asking you to be excessively nice to the point of being perceived as patronising, I am though inviting you to give someone the credit they deserve for their efforts beyond what they could reasonably be expected to do. Equally, there is a time where reprimanding unacceptable behaviour and/or performance can also lead to a positive outcome.

"Being up the creek without a paddle sounds like it could be fun. When do we go?"

Well-meaning but insincere

Leaders often espouse the need for their teams to 'go the extra mile' – a phrase that is intended to reflect the need to put that little more effort into their work, to deliver excellence, get the job done better, and more quickly while eradicating poor quality. These speeches, intended to be motivational and to mobilise the troops can, if relationships are positive, prove highly effective. However, have you ever witnessed a well meaning boss attempt to deliver a well prepared but insincere speech intended to energise a team, only for their message to fall on deaf ears and lead to a lack of trust and respect for the boss? If you haven't witnessed this to date, given time you no doubt will.

The level of motivation within an organisation or team is ultimately set by the leader and their top team. At board level, this is the CEO and those directly reporting to him or her. In a department, this is the head of department and their direct reports. Front-line employees look directly to the behaviour and standards of their managers for motivation. If they are positive, most are likely to follow the example; if negative, it would be misguided for any leader or manager to expect great results.

Fairness, together with open, honest dialogue and mutual respect are ingredients to enhance motivation for individuals and teams. Without these, an organisation is likely to suffer in terms of quality, commitment, productivity and even short-term absenteeism where the key reason for absence is little more than lack of personal motivation.

> *'Flatter me, and I may not believe you. Criticise me, and I may not like you. Ignore me, and I may not forgive you. Encourage me, and I will not forget you. Love me and I may be forced to love you.'*
> William Arthur Ward

Removal of threat-based motivation

While leadership, management and team development approaches continue to evolve, sadly, one approach that continues to appear in organisations is threat-based motivation. This encompasses the in-your-face commands to team members, as well as the far more subtle approach using comments and questions designed to produce fear and subsequently 'encourage' the victim to undertake a specific task or improve productivity.

Let's call it the 'Well, I know you work all the extra hours you can BUT the boss insists we all do more' syndrome. Or how about the 'I know that you have performed really well BUT if you truly want that promotion the boss says you need to do even better' ego-based approach? Such influencing may result in a short-term improvement in productivity but, in the long-term, errors and complaints increase, while trust, respect and support for the manager disappear, and rarely do they return.

Deliver a fair performance appraisal interview

The performance appraisal interview is an opportunity to review an individual's performance and make plans for future development. Employees tend to feel motivated when their efforts have been acknowledged and appreciated, both informally on a day-to-day basis through effective management and also via a formal personal development mechanism such as the appraisal interview.

The performance appraisal interview is an ideal opportunity not only to review past and plan future development goals but also to reinforce the psychological contract between manager and team member. However, it is essential that managers enter the performance appraisal process already having a positive win-win relationship with the appraisee. Problems can arise when such an interview is being undertaken where both parties simply do not trust, respect or communicate effectively with each other. The performance appraisal interview is a wonderful opportunity to nurture working relationships with employees and help them develop both inside and outside the working environment.

Some individuals need to receive regular feedback in order to know that they are performing well. Others know it without being told. As a generalisation, we can say that people are either driven by external or internal feedback. You may have realised already that different people need different levels of feedback.

The easiest way to touch both groups is by stating your feedback like this: 'I know that you don't need me to tell you this, but I really appreciated what you did...'
This way the people who need external feedback will receive your praise and the people who are driven by internal feedback will think 'I know' and feel validated.

Something to think about...

- ✓ Set an example that will inspire others to follow, based on integrity as well as technical skill.

- ✓ Praise employees for their efforts and achievements.

- ✓ Nurture open, honest and trust-based relationships where everybody can contribute and feel appreciated.

- ✓ Dare to be wrong occasionally and acknowledge it. Employees admire authenticity in a leader.

- ✓ Go back to the floor occasionally to understand the challenges your employees face day to day.

- ✓ Act in an authentic manner with honest dialogue being a priority in all of your dealings.

- ✓ Ask people good questions to engage and involve colleagues where possible or practical. You could be pleasantly surprised just how many good ideas they have.

- ✓ Reprimand poor performance privately and with an abundance of integrity – stay away from imposing your seniority and deal with the human being, not the job title.

- ✓ Delegate some of your workload to team members. Help them learn and expand their skills and expertise while demonstrating trust and respect for them.

My Notes

CHAPTER 6:
DEVELOPING EFFECTIVE TEAMWORK

'We value teamwork' – are you sure about that?

Much has been written about the need to develop teamwork within organisations in order to add value to the customer proposition. Indeed, many corporate values statements include 'We value teamwork' as a key attribute; but this statement is very easily said but more challenging to prove in real terms.

How can I develop a team culture in my organisation?

The good thing is, even if you are starting from scratch, with some creative thinking and an in-depth understanding of your people, you can make positive strides forward to develop a team culture. Of course, there are numerous factors that influence the success of a team – far too many to mention in this chapter – but in my experience you can start to turn your dream into reality by first of all understanding and then consistently applying the principles detailed in this book.

Honest, credible leadership

The overriding factor that influences the success of a team is honest, credible leadership. This can be defined as a leadership style that supports the creation of a trusting, mutually supportive and accountable environment, where everybody's unique contribution is both recognised and valued. The usual 'can do' attitude moves on a further step to a 'will do' attitude where honest, credible leaders are in place and team members truly engaged.

Few things destroy team spirit faster than a leader choosing to be economical with the truth or making promises to the team he or she either can't or won't keep. Whether it be making promises to appease team members during a challenging time, or in an effort to reinforce personal popularity, once team members realise that their leader is choosing dishonesty to influence them they are likely to withdraw emotionally and be on their guard when communicating with the leader in future. Ultimately, everybody suffers.

Set a clear context from the outset

Do your team members really understand what they are being asked and trusted to deliver in terms of results? Are they aware of the support they will receive in order to assist them in delivering high quality, worthwhile outcomes? If not, the results achieved are likely to be little more than disappointing, and team motivation and relationships will soon start to suffer. The same principle applies for your organisations' financial performance.

When team members understand what they are being asked to do, know how they are expected to contribute, and then feel supported in making that contribution towards a worthwhile goal they will, in most cases, perform extremely well. Even when facing a tough challenge, they remain solution-focused in their thinking and with the success of the team in mind. Their commitment to the success of the team overall is reinforced by a realisation that they act for everybody's benefit and that their personal contribution is appreciated and worthwhile.

"Also, I'm very good at getting along with incompetent losers."

Develop competence across the team

With the best context in the world, results will be limited without the presence of competent team members or, at least, team members with a desire to reach a level of competency that adds value to the team overall. Indeed, one critical attribute of a high performing team is its willingness to openly share knowledge with others and build its own knowledge bank, where everyone can feel valued for their personal contribution. With this approach, as one team member becomes more competent, so do others.

Not only does an organisation need team members who have the requisite range of skills and expertise but, just as important is the people side of the competence equation. Do the team members actually get along with each other? Can they be relied upon to deal with any problems privately and with a clear focus on keeping the team objectives in mind, rather than becoming involved in office politics and defending their corner?

Crucially, they need to be both able and willing to develop strong personal relationships with internal and external customers that will serve to deliver high quality results. These personal qualities do get noticed by those they come into contact with and the level of trust and respect developed can be breathtaking.

Look for learning opportunities everywhere

When something goes wrong within a team, it can be easy to jump immediately into blaming others for the problem or mistake. Of course, we are all emotional beings who care about getting things right but the true test of a team comes along when something doesn't go to plan. Whatever the situation, once it has been resolved and the project put back on track, where is your focus? Is it on reflecting that perhaps the person wasn't really right for the job, and he or she shouldn't be really trusted again on this type of project? Or is it on understanding how the problem manifested itself, learning from it and working on ensuring that in future, there are better ways of working together and maximising success?

Again, open and honest relationships are key to team success and a great learning opportunity. Part of the learning is giving people permission to be disappointed and upset, however, with a clear context that problems are resolved privately, quickly and with a focus on strengthening the cohesiveness of the team and results achieved together in the future.

Going out to win v Going out not to lose

There is a vast gulf in mindset between going out to win and going out not to lose. The first approach inspires confidence, team spirit and shared accountability where, even when facing defeat, individuals perform at their very best for their own benefit and also for the overall benefit of the team. The 'going out not to lose' mindset is more of a survival mechanism where just doing OK is perceived to be acceptable. This lowers our hopes and expectations and therefore impacts our emotional state, so we don't perform anywhere near our real potential.

Just as some people and teams have a deep fear of failure, the same is also true where some are afraid of succeeding. Take for example a typical sporting scenario – if the underdogs succeed, perhaps they will enjoy the adulation of an adoring and proud nation in the short-term. But, the downside is that the nation now has a very high expectation of them, and they are then under pressure to succeed even more in the future.

Developing a winning team spirit

Teams can definitely be taught how to develop and enhance a winning team spirit, although a winning spirit is a great place to start but a bad place to finish. A team must have a level of technical competence that allows them to perform to a standard that reflects their standing within an organisation. Positive thinking is one thing, but positive doing is an entirely different matter.

The role of the manager is crucial to developing a winning team spirit. If the manager leads by example and sets high standards that the team members are happy and even proud to adhere to, that's great. There may be occasions where a team feels that a manager has not effectively addressed a colleague who is underperforming and this can cause a severe drop in commitment and productivity. In fact, the best managers are those who are not only technically competent but are consistently able to stir up a positive and powerful emotional state in their team, create a laser like focus on the achievement of the desired goal and mobilising everyone to play their part and do what is best for the team and organisation.

Teams that consistently perform at the highest level tend to have a clear understanding of individual team members' strengths and weaknesses, and a clear context of how the team will operate in terms of relationships, support mechanisms and also, how they will deal with problems when they arise. What steps can you take to ensure that your team consistently performs at the highest level?

Something to think about...

- ✓ Understand that new teams develop through experience. There are likely to be growing pains – so be aware that they will happen, and have a strategy for dealing with them in a way that serves to reinforce team purpose and commitment.

- ✓ Ensure that team goals are understood and agreed by everyone involved so that excellent results are the norm and not the exception.

- ✓ Be honest, supportive and set a clear context of agreed standards and expectations for the team's performance.

- ✓ Understand that problems will arise, mistakes will be made and there is a learning opportunity that will serve you well as your team evolves.

- ✓ Take the opportunity to change the shape of the team with individuals taking on different roles and responsibilities to help the team develop new strengths and address weaknesses.

- ✓ Delegate responsibility for decision making as often as possible within a context of competence and accountability – this expression of trust will help team members own their results and develop trust and confidence.

My Notes

CHAPTER 7:
WHY VALUES-DRIVEN ORGANISATIONS STAND OUT FROM THE CROWD

The 21st century has already witnessed a number of corporate scandals which have served as disturbing reminders that, however large or small an organisation is in terms of number of employees or financial turnover, dishonesty really is a personal choice.

Scandals such as Enron and Parmalat are real-life examples of what can happen when the values of the organisation are not actively demonstrated on a daily basis, from the top executive right down to the shop floor workers. It can also be extremely costly – think Barings Bank and Nick Leeson. The once omnipotent Barings was acquired by ING Bank for just £1 as a result of corporate values and operating standards being ignored and a quest for financial profit overshadowing good corporate governance.

On a more positive note, there are many examples of outstanding results being achieved, due to executives choosing to demonstrate a style of leadership grounded in technical competence while also being driven by strong personal values. Sir Richard Branson's airline, Virgin Atlantic, springs immediately to mind. The organisation has a clear vision on how to care for employees, customers and an unswerving commitment to fairness, high quality and loyalty.

Microsoft is another example of an enterprise not afraid to publish its core values on its extensive web site for all to see. Here's what they have to say.

Microsoft Values
As a company, and as individuals, we value:
- Integrity and honesty
- Passion for customers, for our partners, and for technology
- Openness and respectfulness
- Taking on big challenges and seeing them through
- Constructive self-criticism, self-improvement, and personal excellence
- Accountability to customers, shareholders, partners, and employees for commitments, results, and quality

Corporate values can make or break an organisation

Corporate values are clearly important, yet in many organisations they either can't be seen or are not made public. They might be invisible but they remain critical to survival, rather like the oxygen in the air we breathe.

Take a moment to think what the values of your organisation are. If you are fortunate, your corporate values will be made clear to you in some published form and, hopefully and just as importantly, through the way in which business is conducted on a routine basis. Among the key words you may find within a listing of most corporate values include concepts like trust, integrity, teamwork, social responsibility, diversity and equality.

What about other equally important values that somehow most organisations, and individuals for that matter, tend to overlook? What would happen if organisations listed freedom, adventure, fun and creativity amongst their desired list of corporate values? How could relationships and performance flourish as a direct result of employees knowing that their employer considered these values to be of great importance?

Making this knowledge available would tend to attract bright, committed, innovative and creative people – the type of people who invariably drive an organisation towards success by their very outlook and nature. Such recruits are like gold-dust, yet published corporate values don't seek to attract them, except in very rare circumstances.

And how does your organisation interpret its core values? Does it live and breathe them as it should, or do the values exist simply to support an attractive 'mission statement' or to spruce up the annual report and accounts booklet for the benefit of investors? Independent of what the core values are, the organisation that ignores them does so at its peril.

As an example of where ignoring corporate values can have dire results, consider WorldCom. Formed and led by Bernard Ebbers, a former milkman and junior high school basketball coach, WorldCom moved from being a small time player in the telecommunications market to America's second-biggest long-distance telephone company and the largest mover of internet traffic. At its height it was valued at $180 billion and employed over 80,000 people worldwide. For reasons associated with a loss of trust in the organisation, investor confidence collapsed, and the rest as they say, is history.

As an exercise in why values are important, compare the WorldCom scenario with that at GE led at the time by Jack Welch, when one of their managers was involved in an aircraft engine bribery scandal. The organisation is said to have disciplined not only the individual directly involved, but also a whole raft of additional personnel, including some very senior executives with otherwise impeccable records who, they determined, should have detected and averted the wrongdoing. Some may consider this action draconian, but the bottom line was that it sent a very positive signal through a huge operation that protecting the collective integrity and organisational values were critically important.

Personal values are also important

Personal values are a basic statement of what is most important to us as human beings. Traits such as honesty, loyalty, integrity, contribution and generosity are some of the values that make up the core of our beliefs about ourselves and how we want other people to perceive us.

We tend to judge other people on the basis of our own personal values, not theirs

It is also important to note that in any relationship, either inside or outside of the work environment, we tend to judge other people on the basis of our own personal values, not theirs. And, without a clear context being set and actively reinforced by executives and their top leadership team, conflict can occur when people feel that their own personal values are being transgressed. This can result in what I call 'personal withdrawal'.

Personal withdrawal is a lack of personal commitment to activities and tasks, a loss of motivation usually occurring when a person feels that his or her values have been transgressed – often when he or she has been placed in a position of being obliged to perform a task or lead a project which conflicts with his or her own personal values. Withdrawal is rarely a purely intellectual choice, having more to do with the internal conflict created through the negative emotional energy and physical stress caused by transgressing personal values.

In extreme circumstances this can be so severe that for some individuals it becomes virtually impossible for them to maintain their work performance. Ultimately, quality, efficiency and relationships suffer. The many benefits that an organisation can gain from aligning their corporate mission with their employees' values cannot be emphasised strongly enough. When every employee in an organisation feels that they share a common value with their executive team and managers, the results achieved in terms of teamwork, authentic communication, customer satisfaction and financial performance can be outstanding.

Hiring values–driven employees

My own company has witnessed many recruitment programmes where an organisation advertises vacancies with details of remuneration and benefits together with phrases such as "You must be a team player", "willing to go the extra mile" and such like; each statement is clearly a reflection of the qualities the employer is looking for. However, corporate recruitment programmes rarely mention personal or organisational values. But how often do you see phrases like, "You must share our corporate values of honesty, integrity, service and quality?" Possibly not often enough.

One key question rarely asked by an interview panel is "What qualities do you value most in people you work with and why?" This question can lead the conversation in a whole new, far more productive direction and allow the recruiter to understand the applicant's personal values and how they fit (or not) with those of the organisation. By using personal values-driven interview techniques, alongside competency-based techniques, recruiters can reduce recruitment costs, attract people who are passionate about their work and genuinely committed to doing their best, rather than simply turning up to do a job. Customers are also likely to notice a very positive difference and, in many cases, may be eager to follow the example demonstrated by employees on behalf of the organisation they are trusted to represent.

Start with the executive team

You could be surprised at just how much employees know about their leadership team

If employees on the shop-floor are to live their personal values more often and add even more value to your organisation, the executive team needs to lead by example. You could be surprised at just how much employees know about their leadership team. Whether in a negative or positive sense, their perceptions are created by what they believe their leadership team stands for, and against.

By setting a clear context with employees about what qualities the organisation values and then actively demonstrating those qualities on a day-to-day basis, the leader sets standards and permission for others to do the same. Some of the many improvements I have witnessed include enhanced teamwork, efficiency, quality and communication following the sharing of personal values and designing a plan of how a shared vision could be created to ensure that everyone in the organisation moves forward together and with everybody's best interests at heart.

The biggest challenge can be when dealing with an underperforming employee – where colleagues perceive that leaders are 'going easy' on or failing to address a problem with a persistent offender. This too can lead to colleagues withdrawing emotionally if they feel their personal values are being transgressed.

Who you are is just as important as what you sell

The values that an organisation stands for are increasingly affecting their ability to hire the best people and sell their products and/or services. People are becoming increasingly aware of the link between environmental and social issues and how organisations do business. There is an increasing recognition that the days of autocratic leadership and hidden agendas are numbered. There is far too much at stake for it to be otherwise.

Scott Watson

Successful business leaders of the 21st century will be those who find a balance between the interests of the organisation, the interests of the employees and the interests of society as a whole. To achieve this goal they will need to take account of the shift in values taking place in society, and the growing demand for people to find meaning and purpose in their work. It is widely accepted that only by doing this will employees feel relaxed and comfortable enough to perform well and allow their individual flair, innovation and creativity to shine through.

One of the main reasons that organisations are unable to mine the creative potential of their employees is that they fail to understand the importance of linking the personal wellbeing and fulfilment of their employees to that of fulfilling the organisations aspirations. When the link between effort and emotional reward is broken, and employees are paid to do rather than to think, there is no incentive to achieve optimal performance. It is only when employees feel a direct link between their own personal contribution, the success of the organisation and their personal reward that they feel they have a responsibility for the whole. When this happens they feel encouraged to fulfil their potential. In other words, establishing equilibrium between the ethical and economic is essential for a culture that nurtures innovation and creativity and taps human potential on an ongoing basis.

Authentic, values-driven leadership will result in employees following their leaders through desire rather than obligation. The impact on an organisation can be immensely powerful and sustainable when done correctly. So why not sit down with your leadership and management teams and consider how to set a new standard for your organisation and inspire your employees to follow you with passion and purpose? It really can be achieved if you want it to happen.

Something to think about...

- ✓ What benefits could be realised by everyone having an awareness of colleagues' personal values and how they demonstrate them?

- ✓ How could team performance be enhanced if people demonstrated their personal values more often for everybody's benefit?

- ✓ How could some conflict situations be avoided or resolved if there was team awareness and an understanding of others' personal values?

- ✓ How can the personal values of others be highlighted, understood and appreciated?

- ✓ Do you know what the core values of your organisation are, and can you support them wholeheartedly? If not, take a few moments to explore this and check your understanding.

Scott Watson

My Notes

CHAPTER 8:
LEADING BY EXAMPLE

There is a story about Mahatma Gandhi which beautifully reflects the value of leaders not merely setting, but also living the kind of example they would wish others to follow.

A mother brought her young son to see Gandhi as she was worried by her son's high consumption of sugar. She wanted Gandhi to instruct her son to cease this unhealthy habit immediately and expected that the appointment with the wise old man would take just a few minutes. Bemused by Gandhi declining to instruct her child, she nevertheless agreed to his request that she bring her son back to meet with him again the following week. One week later she returned with her son and Gandhi told the child "Stop eating sugar." One month later, the mother returned to Gandhi to share her excitement and joy that her son had in fact stopped eating sugar. Upon asking Gandhi why he could not simply have given the instruction at their first meeting he responded, "Lady, when we first met, I was still eating sugar."

There is a big difference between believing you are an effective leader and actually being an effective leader

Does the same principle apply in your organisation? Do you as a leader set an example that your peers and subordinates genuinely wish to follow not only in terms of technical competence and expertise, but in the way you act and communicate on a daily basis? There is a big difference between believing you are an effective leader and actually being an effective leader. Effective leadership is not measured by a positive performance appraisal and financial bonus reflecting your contribution to the achievement of corporate goals. It takes knowledge, purpose, focus, kindness and an unswerving commitment to both the team and the task – a balance that is often found to be lacking in organisations, but which can be addressed through effective leadership.

Effective leadership in action

Consider for a moment what others have historically achieved through vision and leadership. How about Isambard Kingdom Brunel?

At a time when over 95% of the population of the United Kingdom travelled on foot or by horse, Brunel constructed an almost perfectly level railway line between London and Bristol using technologies that were unproven and almost unheard of at the time. That the railway line is still in use today is a testament to his abilities not just as a skilled engineer but as a leader, because his workforce believed in him and in the goal he had set.

Fast forward to the present day and think about Professor Muhammad Yunus and his Grameen Bank in Bangladesh. Here is a spectacular example of leadership helping to lift millions of people out of poverty and improving their quality of life by offering micro-loans to the poorest members of society based on mutual trust, accountability, participation and creativity – parameters sometimes overlooked in the corporate world. As of December, 2006, the Grameen Bank had nearly 7 million borrowers, 97% of whom are women and a network of over 2300 branches in Bangladesh, providing services in 74,462 villages. Incredible and wonderful. But what is perhaps most surprising is that this organisation boasts a loan repayment rate of 99%. And all because one person had the vision and leadership skills to make it happen and then led by example.

"I have some great new leadership ideas I want you to find inspiring."

There are of course those leaders who do not make the headlines but who do sterling work nevertheless. True leaders are not necessarily the individuals you see on television every day reporting the latest excellent bottom line performance despite challenging markets. Indeed, the most effective leaders are often well kept secrets that calmly go about their business, leading their teams and achieving wonderful things in a spirit of partnership and collaboration. The true bottom line is that good leaders, independent of their status, know how to lead an organisation or team in an honest, ethical and competent manner and, as a result, maintain high levels of performance at individual and team levels. For these people, going the extra mile is more the norm rather than the exception.

Scott Watson

Leadership with purpose

People are really good at spotting authenticity in leaders. For example, during an event for a National Health Service Trust I was invited to present at, the event sponsor – a woman who had risen through the ranks to the level of Director of Nursing – spoke passionately to her audience, each audience member being a nurse having daily and direct contact with patients. She made a simple yet powerful statement that was truly inspiring. Her statement, delivered in a quiet, purposeful manner was: "I know that nursing can sometimes be a stressful job, but please, if there is one standard I ask of each of you, it's that you care for every patient in our hospital as if they are your own mum or dad." Such a plea delivered in isolation may have fallen on deaf ears, however, as this woman was highly respected and trusted by her colleagues for being a fair, honest and caring boss, her statement struck a chord with the audience at a deep emotional level.

This leader realised that if targets are to be achieved, she must first care for and support the very people who are entrusted to achieve those targets. This, in a highly pressurised environment where the personal touch can be overlooked due to conflicting priorities, shows that effective leaders can create a common purpose and an environment where colleagues actually want to become involved and contribute to the success of their organisation.

As another example of leadership with purpose, reflect on the mission of Mother Teresa of Calcutta. Did she present any problems with authenticity of purpose? I think not. Small wonder that her colleagues, together with millions of people across the world, supported her willingly and with the sense of commitment that only comes from being associated with a great leader endeavouring to accomplish great deeds. The most effective leaders, as well as being competent in their role, connect at the deepest level with those they lead. Their impact is often overwhelmingly positive and reaches beyond the normal intellectual part of us and truly touches our hearts. How many hearts have you connected with or touched this week? How many hearts can you connect with today, tomorrow, next week and next month? If you truly wish to become an effective leader with a sense of purpose that others will recognise, this is one area where you may have some work to do.

The value of open, honest feedback

The value of open, honest feedback cannot be underestimated. Without this kind of support and guidance we cannot grow as human beings. But who is going to feel comfortable or confident in providing some 'tough love' to a boss who ultimately may have a heavy influence over his or her future career prospects and job security? For such feedback to be given and also received in a productive manner, the relationship must be solid and based on mutual trust and respect.

It is not that good leaders don't make mistakes – it is that they openly acknowledge that they have indeed made a mistake and realise that the best way to achieve their goals is to have a cohesive team based as much on strong personal values and open, honest dialogue as well as technical expertise. Leadership also isn't about always having the right answers to every question. It is however about mobilising resources to achieve worthwhile if not challenging goals.

When the relationship between leaders and team members is packed full of open, honest dialogue, where employees on the front line respect their managers for their competence and integrity rather than for the status or seniority they hold in a structure chart, an organisation will be able to flourish. The absence of such standards can ultimately destroy an organisation. The stakes are very high, so could it be worth investing some effort to ensure you get it right?

Scott Watson

Moving beyond approval seeking

There are many reasons why people actively seek approval from their immediate manager or peers. It may be a desire to feel appreciated or valued, to demonstrate competence in a new skill, or for it to be recognised that the level of performance required has been met. Approval seeking in isolation can though, become unhealthy when individuals need to achieve recognition through the good opinions of others (usually more senior). Worse still, when obtaining approval becomes the key influence that drives whether an individual performs brilliantly or badly, even the most effective training and appraisal systems will not be able to address the imbalance.

What is needed is an environment that recognises good performance as one facet of teamwork, but also maintains the focus very clearly on achieving the task and how an individual has and can continue to contribute. When working with corporate executives, I find time after time that the people who attract most approval are those who, perhaps paradoxically, do not actually seek it. These individuals, in addition to being competent in their role, are motivated and driven by their knowledge, their personal values, and sense of purpose. And, there are those who do not give other people's good (or bad) opinions of them a second thought. When they receive positive feedback on their standard of work or commitment to achieving a tight deadline, they will always accept a genuine "thank you" or "well done" and that is enough for them.

Rarely will they accept other people's opinions of them as a statement of fact, even when being told how wonderful they are. In short, they have transcended the need for their ego to be stroked and are operating independently of the opinions of others. They are free from many of the constraints, problems and difficulties that surround many of their colleagues. How many leaders do you know who operate in this manner? Perhaps there is a leadership lesson for you and your colleagues to explore together?

Leaders have a wonderful opportunity to influence, even inspire the people they are employed and trusted to lead. Perhaps there is a lot of truth in Gandhi's statement "You must be the change you wish to see in the world." Would it not be a wonderful experience for everyone if more leaders dared to bring some humanity back in to organisations? The opportunity for you to move towards a more effective and even inspiring leadership style exists at this very moment. Why not take a chance and really go for it?

Something to think about...

- ✓ What are your three most positive attributes/qualities as a leader?

    a)

    b)

    c)

- ✓ How do these attributes/qualities help you to win hearts and minds among your team?

- ✓ Who in your team could you ask for some candid feedback to create some awareness of potential blind spots that perhaps don't support your efforts to be a highly effective leader?

My Notes

CHAPTER 9:
KINDNESS – THE MISSING PIECE OF THE CORPORATE JIGSAW

In the rush to hit tough performance targets and deliver improved results – often with fewer resources – keeping employees actively engaged in their work has never been more vital. But, even in an era that has brought so many technological advances, the one beautifully simple attribute so often overlooked in organisations is kindness.

The word kindness itself probably does not appear in more than one corporate mission statement in every thousand. And, perhaps only a similar proportion of readers will have considered it to be a useful factor in the operation of a successful organisation or team. There is clearly scope for advances to be made, and you may find it really valuable to reflect on the text that follows and judge for yourself just how powerful kindness can be when introduced meaningfully into our working lives.

If you are thinking that kindness is not measurable, and therefore not worthy of a mention on your mission or corporate values statements, you are missing out on something which has the potential to greatly enhance the performance of your operation, no matter how big or small. Kindness is also free and can, like a smile, be shared with others while still being retained by the originator. Few things in life posses such fantastic attributes.

I just have to help

The ability to act in a spirit of kindness is within each and every one of your colleagues, and you too

What is it that convinces us to act in a spirit of true kindness? Sadly, it is all too often a horrific experience that connects with us as human beings at the deepest level, beyond our intellectual brain, going directly to our heart. Remember the outpouring of public kindness and generosity following the terrible events of 11th September 2001, and the Asian tsunami of Christmas 2004, when the world woke up to witness such a terrible tragedy for those who lost their lives and their loved ones left behind. Who among us wasn't touched by the horrific scenes we viewed on our television screens, and who didn't experience a profoundly authentic, deeply personal desire to help in some way?

And what about acts of kindness that impact on us at a personal level when it involves a loved one? It happened to me recently and certainly reinforced my belief that kindness is one of the most important facets of our often complex lives that we unwittingly ignore to our detriment. Permit me to share the circumstances with you.

Much has been written about the many challenges faced within our National Health Service in terms of budget cuts, under-resourcing, staffing issues and ward closures, together with their impact on the quality of patient care. Just before writing this chapter I witnessed first hand on a very personal basis, nursing and support staff in my local hospital responding unstintingly to the needs of their patients, each patient experiencing their own very personal challenges and for some, fears about their lives coming to an end. One such patient was my mother.

Scott Watson

Among the daily pressures of running their section of the hospital in an effective manner, the nursing staff demonstrated so many random acts of kindness that lifted the atmosphere throughout the entire ward. Nothing complex, but crucially important things like a kind smile or finding a few precious moments to gently encourage my mother to try and eat some food to build up her strength, as well as giving both her (and me) a reassuring hug at particularly difficult times. Their efforts in supporting my mother, and indirectly other family members through a traumatic time, were moments of pure inspiration and one of the best possible demonstrations imaginable of the impact of kindness in action.

Kindness is within us all

The ability to act in a spirit of kindness is within each and every one of your colleagues, and you too. Unfortunately, this special part of us often remains hidden away as other people may sometimes perceive random acts of kindness as a sign of weakness when the exact opposite is true.

Daring to express genuine kindness towards another human being, whether in the middle of emotional turmoil and conflict, or even when all is going well, is a demonstration of strength at its purest level. A genuine 'well done' or 'thank you' can work wonders in an organisation. The authentic act of kindness has a domino effect on colleagues and suppliers and can positively impact on the quality of care you provide to your customers. Kindness works for the greater good so that everybody benefits.

Don't believe it? I once had the good fortune to be shown around a leisure complex that had a reputation for treating everyone well. As part of the tour, the director I was with introduced me to the lady who cleaned the toilets. That was unusual in itself. More unusual was the fact that it became clear from our brief discussion that she considered herself to be a valued member of the operation. When I privately put this to the director, he commented that if both he and she failed to turn up for work tomorrow, she would most certainly be missed first, and most! With such acknowledgement of the importance of people's roles in an organisation, no wonder this enterprise was very successful in its chosen market.

Complex structure; simple principle

Despite organisations being complex in structure, the principle that supports kindness, meaning and purpose is simplicity itself. From the foster mum I was honoured to coach, who has dedicated her life to caring for over three hundred children who told me "Scott, this is the work I was born to do and there's nothing in this world stronger than unconditional love," through to the florist who in addition to creating a masterpiece with every bouquet she designs, cares so much about her customers as human beings, they just keep coming back to her for more. Even though there are many florists offering flowers, she gives something much more. Kindness!

At the corporate level it isn't about having your CEO pictured with a donation cheque in the newspapers. Donating to community or international charitable projects is a wonderful habit and standard to possess but there needs to be a balance between making charitable donations and treating your employees with kindness too. When was the last meeting you attended that demonstrated a random act of kindness? I understand that kindness often only appears when a colleague has suffered serious illness or the loss of a loved one – but how about committing to demonstrating kindness on a daily basis?

So how does kindness work in the often robust and aggressive corporate jungle? Well, random acts of kindness can energise employees and transform a workplace from one where people undertake work to one where people really want to do their best. The difference in performance can be staggering.

The late Anita Roddick, founder of The Body Shop, espoused the value of kindness in companies through her book, A

Revolution in Kindness, asking what the world would look like if we all valued basic human kindness above other values. Ms Roddick successfully twinned entrepreneurship with kindness on a massive scale. So too can your organisation. The results will be much more impressive than you could possibly imagine.

Those organisations with a more compassionate, humane approach to leading and supporting their people in a spirit of genuine kindness, collaboration, and commitment, are generally more trusted by their customers, employees and even investors. They also generally happen to be very successful in what they do. Strange then that compassion, forgiveness and understanding are not generally exposed or included in any debate or discussion on how organisations are run and how profit is generated.

An equally well known and frequently overlooked fact is that eliminating or ignoring these factors can have the exact opposite effect at every level in any organisation. Be it an important board room debate or simply a minor departmental meeting, self-serving agendas twinned with ego-based bravado can serve to destroy the very foundations on which truly successful organisations can be built.

So how do we incorporate kindness into our daily working lives and reap the rich benefits and rewards it has to offer?

Creating meaning and purpose

When Mabel is making widgets, it might be misguided to expect her to care after the first 10,000 drop onto the conveyor belt. But when she understands that her widgets will be incorporated into a device used for helping disabled children to walk, it becomes a whole new ballgame. You can bet that Mabel will begin to understand and appreciate the value of her personal contribution to a cause that is not only worthwhile but also making a positive contribution to the quality of lives of other human beings. When meaning and purpose underpin an individual's job role their focus changes from 'earning' to 'serving', and they are always more than willing to go the extra mile through a sense of altruism above any other factor.

These attitudes to work, whereby we transcend our ego and open up to more open, honest and authentic dialogue need to prevail throughout organisations if they are to become truly successful in a sustainable manner. It is regrettable that the higher up the corporate ladder one moves, the more difficult it can become to change the operational ethos. Words like compassion, forgiveness, kindness and understanding are generally not routinely bandied about in the boardroom. This is unfortunate, because, if an organisation is to move forward, it is here where change must start and from where it must be driven.

Kindness in action

Random acts of kindness don't just reflect well on the reputation of an organisation, they leave a lasting impression on the people lucky enough to receive them

Let us return for a moment if we may to the hospital mentioned earlier in this chapter. The key factor that I witnessed among the nursing staff caring for my mother was that each communication was delivered in such a genuine and loving manner that it connected not so much with a patient with a life-threatening illness, but as a human being with her own feelings deserving of respect and understanding. This also works just as effectively at the corporate level. Random acts of kindness don't just reflect well on the reputation of a person or their organisation, they leave a lasting impression on the people lucky enough to receive them. Kindness costs nothing yet it can accomplish great things. Random acts of kindness are never wasted; each act creates an abundance of positive feelings and goodwill that expands almost without effort.

Scott Watson

So what would you rather be remembered for? What you accumulated in terms of salary package, company car and pension, or the imprints you made in other people's hearts and minds? Remembering and practising kindness will very likely enable you to accomplish both.

Something to think about...

- ✓ If you have the chance to be right or to be kind, choose kind.

- ✓ A genuine 'thank you' or 'well done' can take up to five seconds. Find time each day to have this dialogue.

- ✓ Begin and end each day with an attitude of gratitude. Remember all of the things in your life you have to be grateful for.

- ✓ Ensure your colleagues understand how their contribution adds value to a meaningful cause, just like Mabel.

- ✓ Give because you want to give and not because you expect a thank you.

- ✓ Change your focus from earning to serving. It is transformational.

- ✓ Practise random acts of kindness towards other human beings on a daily basis.

This chapter is dedicated to the wonderful men and women of Calderdale Royal Hospital, Ward 6B whose kindness brought so many smiles to my mother's face in the final days of her life. Your kindness is truly inspirational.

Scott Watson

<u>My Notes</u>

CHAPTER 10:
PERFORMANCE APPRAISALS – NECESSARY EVIL OR PRICELESS DEVELOPMENT TOOL?

It is widely accepted in the human resources arena that the performance appraisal system is a crucial part of any organisation's development strategy. Many corporate executives proudly claim that "our people are our most important asset," but an effective performance appraisal process is vital if executives are to turn such bold statements into reality.

But why should an organisation use a performance appraisal system?

The answer is straightforward – If you can't accurately measure the effectiveness of your employees, you will have absolutely no idea of current performance levels, any weaknesses to be addressed or even how to identify what is actually being done well.

The performance appraisal system is a corporate development tool that, done correctly, can add lots of value to the employee being appraised as well as the employer. It provides a rare opportunity to talk about, not just **what** they do, but **how** they do it, and serves as an important reference point for every employee to ensure that their understanding and expectations of their performance match those of their employer. For some organisations these issues are only discussed in detail at the recruitment stage, so it is not surprising that a few years down the line, understandings of what is expected may have diverged.

Why performance appraisal systems sometimes fail

There are many reasons. The 'one size fits all' approach to designing the appraisal system itself is a dangerous one to take. If an appraisal process is to work effectively and add value, it needs to be tailored to operate alongside the unique needs of your organisation. But the most important factor is the existing management culture and support systems already in place. In a well-run, effective organisation, the introduction of an appraisal system merely formalises good management support.

A typical situation where an appraisal system would not work well is where it is used as a mechanism for trying to encourage managers to 'manage'. Here, the appraisal system is a way of recording the ongoing performance discussions of an individual and their manager but it is certainly not a substitute for the effective management and supervision of team members.

Absence of trust and credibility can destroy an appraisal interview

For an appraisal interview to be a successful and valuable experience, the appraiser must already have credibility with his or her team. I have observed interviews where it quickly became clear that the absence of trust, respect and open, honest dialogue throughout the review period was resulting in a verbal wrestling match where rapport was destroyed and blame for supposed failures were the order of the day. Can you imagine how badly the next review period was likely to be with such a relationship existing?

Managers sometimes forget that the appraisal interview is not a time for apportioning blame, for addressing all the stored up issues that have occurred during the year, or for telling team members for the first time that the expected level of performance has not been achieved. Such feedback should be dealt with as part of the day-to-day management activities. Where trust and credibility are absent, the performance appraisal process becomes little more than a form-filling exercise that is of no value to the appraisee, appraiser or the organisation.

Lack of planning and care

While the mobile telephone is undoubtedly a valuable piece of technology, for many people it has become a work driver, not an organisational tool. It is important that mobile communications are managed appropriately.

Picture this scene for a moment. Your performance for the previous six months is being appraised by your manager and his mobile phone starts to ring. He stops talking mid sentence to look at who is calling him, looks at you and says with an air of authority, "This call is important, I have to take it but it will only take a few minutes," and then proceeds to talk to the caller about nothing related to work or of any great urgency. Finally, the call comes to an end and the appraiser says "anyway, where were we?" and attempts to remember what he was speaking about before the phone call. How do you feel? This is not a fictional situation; it is an incident that actually happened.

Despite his behaviour, the manager became rather angry when the lady being appraised assertively stated to him "This is exactly how you treat me in the office. You don't listen to what I have to say and then can't even be bothered to remember what we were talking about." She confidently insisted the appraisal interview be postponed and that she would make appropriate notes on the appraisal form regarding his behaviour when the process was finally completed – with the Human Resources Manager in attendance!

Are you that kind of manager? If you are and are appraising colleagues, what level of personal value do you place on them if you answer your phone during what is supposed to be a private, focused and confidential discussion? Please don't take your mobile phone to the appraisal interview, it will only cause problems.

How to achieve the best value from your performance appraisal system

The first step is to understand your organisation's performance appraisal system. If, as a manager, you don't actually understand the purpose or context for the system, how can you deliver it in an authentic manner? Perhaps ask your Human Resources team for some guidance.

1)   Make sure you have a system that supports improved performance

Unfortunately, some performance appraisal systems are poorly designed and implemented. The first step to having an effective system is making sure that the system is fit for purpose. This means that the system actually supports improved performance. Ask yourself a few key questions about the system and whether it encourages:

- ❖ The appraisee to provide an objective self-assessment of their performance?

- ❖ The appraisee to identify the skills and knowledge they would need to improve their performance?

- ❖ The appraiser to provide accurate, objective and positive feedback?

- ❖ The appraiser to assist the appraisee in identifying the most appropriate ways of improving performance?

- ❖ The appraisee and appraiser to build on the experiences of the past to improve the appraisal process?

- ❖ A discussion that focuses on the practicalities of the job role in a language that is understood by both participants?

- ❖ Agreement on action to be taken?

2)   Plan, plan, plan

Plan everything in advance – completing the documentation, booking a quiet meeting room for the discussion, informing the appraisee of the schedule of events and allowing them the opportunity to ask you questions ahead of the discussion.

It is important that you, as the appraiser, value the system and encourage others to do the same. Valuing the system isn't about telling people it is important, it is about demonstrating its importance by the way you communicate and behave. If you treat the appraisal process as an additional piece of useless bureaucracy, then that is exactly what it will become. Conversely, if you treat it as a key organisational development tool designed to improve performance, workplace communication and morale, it will become that too.

3)   Be a credible manager day-to-day

Self-awareness is a great skill to possess. If you have ever been appraised by a manager that you believe lacks credibility in their role, untrustworthy or just plain lazy, you know how it can feel to listen to them give you 'feedback' for an hour on how you must improve during the months ahead if you are to have a successful career. All the time, you were sitting there thinking 'yeah right', and not really listening to what was being said to you.

So, if you are a manager who is trusted to deliver authentic, impartial and objective appraisal interviews, how could you become a more trusted and credible manager on a day-to-day basis? If you don't already know, perhaps it could be valuable to ask several of your team members for some supportive feedback that will help you to grow as a manager? If you are currently managing in a way that is designed to add lots of value to your organisation, you should already be actively inviting open, honest feedback from your team.

One of the key responsibilities for a manager is to spot where people have done a good job and praise them for it as soon as practically possible following the event. Another key role is to discuss substandard performance with staff **when it happens**. Individuals who are learning and growing in their abilities will make mistakes – the key skill of management is how the manager responds to errors and mistakes.

Reprimands should not be the first response to errors; they should be reserved for errors that are repeated, where learning is clearly not taking place. Instead, errors and mistakes should be used as a teaching opportunity, an opportunity to discuss what went wrong, why and how it could be done better next time. If the focus is maintained on the potential for performance improvement and learning, it will help employees to be more open and honest about the mistakes they make and it will help to reduce and resolve them.

For an effective and supportive manager who praises good work and helps staff to reflect on mistakes to improve performance, the appraisal process is documenting the management dialogue that manifests itself within the everyday experience of the appraiser and appraisee.

4) Shut up and listen, really listen

Remember, the purpose of the appraisal interview is to help the appraisee reflect on their performance. While the appraisal interview is really a 'discussion', the majority of the talking may be done by the appraisee, not the appraiser.

One skill I often find missing in organisations is the ability and willingness to actively listen. When people are invited to talk openly, honestly and in a safe environment, it can set a whole new standard for the working relationship between manager and team member. Please, please, please stay away from comments such as "Well I think you should..." and "You know, I once had an experience just like that, and what I did was..." Such comments, however well meaning, take the focus off the appraisee and place it on the appraiser, and this is where ego comes into play. The purpose of the discussion is to focus on the appraisee. Practice the habit of really listening to what your team members are communicating to you and, if you take their open, honest comments as an opportunity to learn, you could help your colleagues to enhance their effectiveness more quickly and easily than you could have imagined.

To be effective at listening you also need highly developed questioning skills. Asking good questions that will encourage appraisees to assess their performance accurately is vital. Remember that learning occurs when the individual discovers the lesson for themselves, hence directing their thinking through carefully crafted questions is central to the process. Brushing up on the questioning skills will reap rewards in the appraisal process.

5) Be honest, it's so much easier to remember

Occasionally, we can inadvertently have a poor impact when communicating with others. Honesty, together with good rapport, is vital if you are to achieve the best possible outcomes from your appraisal interview and help team members become motivated and even excited about the months ahead. Again, if a manager is perceived to be dishonest within the workplace on a day-to-day basis, however honest they claim to be during the appraisal discussion, they are unlikely to be believed.

But, when a productive working relationship exists, you may be pleasantly surprised at just how openly appraisees welcome feedback on their performance and support in designing a bright future. As a manager, as well as having the required technical competence, honesty is the most important attribute you can possess.

6) Base your assessment on fact, not opinion

There may be times when you need to address repeated poor performance during an appraisal discussion. Hence it is crucial that you base all your judgements on evidence. Examples of actual performance should be used to qualify **all comments** on the appraisee. If there are any critical remarks, you should qualify them with examples of actual events to support your statement. Also, if you wish to praise an employee for good work, share a specific example with them. If the appraisee wishes to challenge any of your remarks this will set the standard for such a challenge – they would be expected to provide equivalent evidence to support their claim. Only through a rigorous use of specific examples can you move away from a prejudice and impression-based appraisal to an objective assessment of performance.

My Notes

CHAPTER 11:
IN SEARCH OF ETHICAL LEADERSHIP

Enron was on top of the world. In 2000, it was the seventh biggest company in America. Lauded in the media for being "the most innovative company in the United States", it was considered a successful company run by a high quality management team. But it failed by not making integrity the company's central value.

Once trust is damaged, it is extremely difficult to win back. What Enron executives failed to appreciate was that trust is core to the viability of any organisation. Trust is required for customers to want to buy and for investors to want to invest. When trust disappeared, the value of Enron stocks vanished overnight. A recipient of billions of dollars in loans from banks, Enron quickly found out that the banks not longer trusted it and the whole house of cards came crashing down.

Even in the face of the whirlwind that engulfed them, executives saw it as an exercise in damage control rather than a test of integrity and transparency. What Enron appeared to lack was individual leaders who were prepared to do what is right; to demonstrate genuine leadership and integrity in the face of corporate greed. It needed 'ethical leaders'.

The true leader is someone who concentrates on doing the right thing as well as doing things right

There is no escaping the fact that all social organisations are ethical organisations, in as much as they are decision-making structures that have an impact on people. Leaders and managers are ethical agents who must often make decisions that favour one ethical value over another or one group over another. Indeed, virtually every social arrangement benefits some people at the expense of others; thus, leaders must not only behave responsibly as individuals, but must create an institution where standards of *justice*, *fairness* and *integrity* are upheld and demonstrated; what we could call 'an ethical institution'.

The true leader is someone who concentrates on doing the right thing as well as doing things right. Whether or not they acknowledge it, leaders have a responsibility to exercise the authority they are entrusted with in an ethical way.

What is an ethical leader and how do we spot one?

Ethics is about judgements, so there is no manual or checklist to determine what one needs to do. And, by definition, there is no 'bluffer's guide' either. Ethical leaders are identified and judged by their actions. They have a clear sense of ethical standards, a genuine sense of purpose and an integrity that they act on consistently. They are self-aware and questioning individuals who shape their actions by their need to be true and fair to themselves and to their colleagues.

They often assume that the world would be a better place if people always behaved according to certain widely accepted standards (such as telling the truth). They can examine dilemmas from different perspectives. Some of the key qualities they possess and act on are their abilities to:

- ❖ Anticipate the consequences of actions, identifying who will be affected and in what ways and,

- ❖ Identify how they would like to be treated under similar circumstances (put themselves in the other person's shoes).

Ethical leaders are often those who are able to re-frame ethical issues; frequently able to find a third way, a compromise that avoids the conflict and damage of an either-or decision. But above all, ethical leaders have the habit of conscious reflection; they learn by their experiences.

However, it would be wrong to assume that ethical leaders have a simple choice of good versus bad that merely requires the confidence to act. Often the dilemma for the leader is not a choice between right and wrong, but a choice between two rights. Dilemmas arise when deeply held personal values conflict. Most people when faced with such a dilemma would respond by taking the path of least resistance, by deferring to superiors or taking protection in official policies, or even blaming office politics for their inability to act appropriately. In such situations the ethical leader will carefully judge his or her response based on the best ethical solution, irrespective of the difficulty and obstacles placed in front of him or her.

Ethical organisations

Ethical leadership begins with ethical leaders. Great leaders embody the message they advocate. They are teachers who teach, not just through words, but also through their actions. Only by the establishment of a clear set of ethical standards in the actions of an organisation's leaders can the foundations of an ethical organisation be laid.

It is one area where visions and mission statements, while positive in theory, are meaningless in reality. Subordinates need actually to see evidence of their leaders demonstrating the values through their actions.

A key indicator of an ethical leader is one who uses his or her power – with restraint

Clearly, values such as honesty and integrity are essential to the development of trust. But, in addition to honesty and integrity, the ethical leader must be willing to accept accountability without always attempting to impose control. Ethical leaders acknowledge their own weaknesses and limitations rather than hide behind their given status and power. Indeed, a key indicator of an ethical leader is one who uses his or her power – with restraint.

Becoming an ethical leader

Just as a footballer may develop football skills by playing, people become virtuous by practising virtue. Often, knowing the right thing to do is not difficult, it's doing it that is – through conscious practice, by asking questions such as:

- What do my relationships suggest I do?
- How will this affect others?
- What are my ideals?
- How am I falling short of my ideals?
- What do I need to do to get my ideals back on track?

People often believe that ethical behaviour is reserved for big decisions – but that's not true. Ethical behaviour is for all the small everyday decisions we make in our working and personal life. It is a way to operate, a way to be and a way to encourage success. For an ethical leader, simple human integrity is a constant companion. The good news is that there is an abundance of this powerful, rewarding quality to go around. Everyone can have it, no fee involved. Just take it – it's yours to keep for as long as you want it. But much like any other value or skill, you stand to restrict your success if you fail to apply this standard on a consistent basis.

Scott Watson

Beyond office politics

How often have you attended a meeting with your peers and leader where the purpose is to plan the future growth and prosperity of your organisation?

The brainstorming process begins, the ideas are creative, high energy with laughs and smiles abounding as suggestions are put on the table. But pause and think for just a moment. As you see every face gathered around the table, every department head from sales, customer service to human resources, ask yourself a simple but powerful question. The question that you need to give a simple "Yes" or "No" answer to is: "Is this office filled with ethical leaders?" Remember to include yourself in the group.

If you are involved in office politics or bad relationships, you are playing your part in making it that way. You are also costing your organisation money.

If leaders are to create an environment where well-intended vision, values and mission statements are to be taken seriously, surely, the change needs to be made by corporate leaders taking the first step forward.

Perhaps it would be useful for you and your top team to get together and find out whether you can, with hand on your heart, say that you live your organisation's values. Remember, the true leader is someone who concentrates on doing the right thing, not on doing things right. If you are not already one of them, how about starting from now?

My Notes

CHAPTER 12:
RELATIONSHIPS MAKE THINGS HAPPEN

I once had the great privilege to work with a colleague who was undoubtedly a kindred spirit. I felt comfortable in her company, respected the work she undertook and trusted the outcomes she arrived at. Just as importantly, I knew that she held my knowledge, skills and experience in similar high regard.

Over a period of several years working together, we developed a rapport that remains strong to this day, maintained only through very irregular contact as our career paths diverged and we even lived in different continents for a time. Whenever I felt unsure about how best to proceed with a work related event I knew I could call her for an impartial viewpoint, and she would reciprocate. We still do it today many years down the line.

Such wonderful working relationships are extremely rare, however. For the majority of the time, most of us will have to work with people and organisations where such a rapport does not exist or is very hard if not impossible to build.

Hard to Maintain

Except in rare circumstances like the one mentioned above, relationships can be difficult to create, hard to incubate and even harder to maintain. Why? Simply because relationships are things which exist between people and people are complex entities frequently charged with attempting difficult and often conflicting things as part of their role within an organisation.

Relationships between people, at all levels, are the intangibles that accomplish outcomes, and can result in the success or failure of projects, timescales, outputs and, all too frequently, the very existence of the organisation itself.

It is important to remember that relationships aren't about 'liking' people, although this always helps. Relationships go far beyond liking and can be the glue that binds individuals together through the most challenging of times and almost guarantees the achievement of the most positive outcomes. Think about the recent demise of the classical pop band G4. Despite what they described as frequent internal bickerings and discontent, they played to sell-out theatres, sold several million records and had numerous hits during the past few years. Their working relationships and mutual desire to create music and perform on stage helped them to overcome their likes and dislikes, and permitted them to become extremely successful and perhaps wealthy too.

Trust, Mutual Respect & Integrity

Remember that in organisations while it is nice to work with people we like, it isn't necessary to like people to be able to work with them, providing relationships between you are built on the triple solid foundations of trust, mutual respect and integrity. Customer-Supplier relationships built in this fashion are the ones which survive best despite the vagaries of the marketplace, and in those circumstances when friendships alone cannot overcome problems like late deliveries, poor quality and inadequate service.

One organisation I know demonstrated this to me quite vividly during a recent visit. On a tour of the warehouse I asked why one supplier's goods appeared to be favoured over all others in terms of volumes stocked. The Buyer responded grudgingly by advising that it certainly wasn't because of price, because similar goods were available at a 5% discount. The reason was because the favoured supplier had an excellent and proven long-term track record of keeping their commitments and an excellent relationship with the Buyer on a business basis. Initiatives such as inter-company visits had been organised, the Buyer had access to the supplier's real-time production plans, and deliveries were scheduled when needed, not when the supplier had a spare vehicle. The supplier didn't bother with complex computer based feedback mechanisms; they simply asked the Buyer what was already going well and what else they could do to enhance the already positive relationship. A fast, effective and genuine way to develop a relationship for everybody's benefit.

While the Buyer enjoyed an excellent business relationship with his opposite number, it became apparent that he clearly didn't like him all that much and they seldom socialised. "Dave can be a hard-nut when it comes to pricing and annual contracts," the Buyer advised, "and we frequently don't see eye-to-eye on many issues. If ever we have a problem, however, he's round here like a shot and it gets resolved. I can also rely on him to maintain deliveries, adjust production at his end and ensure we get what we want when we want it so we stick with his company; and his higher prices," he added ruefully. A classic example of trust, respect and integrity overcoming the barriers surrounding the inability of both parties to become friends.

Building Relationships

So how can relationships be created, built, maintained and used to achieve results of mutual benefit? Because relationships are things which exist between people, treating others as you would like to be treated is a good starting place. Show them trust, mutual respect and integrity, value their thoughts, ideas and concepts, and really listen to what they have to say. They obviously feel it is important so give them the space to express their thoughts and feelings. Explain your business position clearly and concisely and don't make promises you can't or won't keep. Until experience proves it to be impossible or irrational, trust the other person and do everything possible to gain his or her trust. Building relationships in this manner is rather like gardening. The ground needs to be prepared, the seeds need to be carefully selected and sown at the appropriate time and they must be tended and nurtured to enable them to grow.

"I'd like to take this opportunity to acknowledge my wonderful coaching, which resulted in your accomplishments."

Regrettably, some weeding will also be necessary because no matter how skilful you are at building relationships in this fashion there will always be those who will endeavour to exploit your good intent and integrity. Know them for what they are, but don't write them off, however, because times, circumstances and people can and do change. View them as a challenge, but proceed with all due caution.

Mutual interests can also help spark the building of a relationship and joint support for, say, the same sports team is frequently a good icebreaker. Paradoxically, the inverse also holds true and friendly if cutting banter about the relative merits of teams can also help a relationship along providing the foundations of the relationship are firmly bedded into the ground and reinforced through time and experience.

Genuine Interest

The mere fact that you are demonstrating genuine interest in the other party and the things that make them tick is a powerful motivator and one of the other essential building blocks of a good relationship. Note, however, the use of the word 'genuine'. If the relationship is to develop and grow, genuine must mean exactly that. Anyone only pretending to be genuine will soon be found out and any embryonic relationship damaged or terminated. I urge you to only ask someone how they are if you are genuinely interested in their response.

And what about some of the other things that you shouldn't do in a relationship? Assigning blame is arguably one of the worst things that you can do. Of course, when things have gone wrong they need to be investigated and appropriate remedial action initiated, but finger pointing never assisted any situation. Remember, when you point a finger at someone else, there are three pointing right back at you.

Holding grudges and exhibiting hostility are similar negative and unhealthy things to do and might blind you to many of the strengths and positives other individuals possess. According to newest studies, we can work as hard and as long as we like as long as we don't harbour feelings of hostility, rancour or bitterness. When things do go wrong, therefore, accept them for what they are, put them right, initiate action to ensure they don't happen again, and move on.

Remember, you can't change the past, only influence the future. How you choose to do this is down to you so please choose wisely.

To conclude, as we spend over half our waking lives at work we really do deserve to have good working relationships while we are there. They will make us, our colleagues, and associates feel more relaxed, content and happy, and will certainly have a very positive impact on the success of individuals and the organisation. Good relationships like this stand out and they will be noticed by customers as well and assist to create a subliminal yet very positive message. Can your organisation really afford to have poor relationships?

Relationships. They're not always easy to create, frequently even harder to maintain, but they're worth it.

Scott Watson

Something to think about…

There will be times in any relationship where disagreements appear and voices are raised. Find the courage to deal with issues fairly and with a sense of kindness and there won't be many problems that can't be overcome.

Deal with the problem at hand rather than dragging up past examples of how this person has mistreated you. Focus on the now.

Take a moment to consider what a good relationship consists of for you. What attributes, standards and values must be included for you to consider it a good relationship?

When you are clear on the above question, why not commit to demonstrate those key attributes, standards and values in all of your relationships on a daily basis – and start to notice how people treat you more positively? Even those people who you just couldn't seem to get along with previously.

Commit to taking some positive steps to resolve a relationship issue that has been ongoing for some time. Remember, leaders should set the example others would wish to follow.

My Notes

CHAPTER 13:
HOW TO USE TRAINING AS AN EMPLOYEE RETENTION TOOL

Many organisations claim to have a commitment to developing their employees. Phrases such as '*our people are our most valuable asset*' are often spotted on motivational posters in companies of all industries and sizes. Furthermore, many directors genuinely believe that this bold statement is true, as do I.

Unfortunately, many executives do not proactively embrace a structured and relevant approach to helping employees at the junior and middle management levels who want to stay with their employer long term. Of course, there are many factors unrelated to training and development that cause people to decide to leave an organisation and explore new opportunities. New career goals, better financial reward and many more factors need to be considered.

But how can you, as a leader, go about implementing an approach to training and development that will not only help your people perform far better than they currently do, but also reinforce the psychological and emotional contracts that are vital to the success of a genuine, sustainable, win-win working relationship?

So many well intended training and development initiatives fail to deliver the results needed by the organisation. In fact, research undertaken by MORI estimated that, in the year 2002, over twelve million UK based workers did not receive any training in the previous year. And guess which budget is often the first to be slashed during a tough trading period? The training and development budget of course.

A structured approach

If executives are to not only attract but also retain and develop a high performing workforce that adds genuine value to the organisation on a consistent basis, a more structured approach is needed when planning and undertaking training and development activities. This requires a change in mind-set at the very top of the organisation.

First, it is important to see employee turnover for what it is – an important part of any organisation. It provides the continual renewal of skills and experience, which in turn acts as a motor for innovation, longevity and sustainability. It is only when this turnover reaches a scale where it begins to have a detrimental effect on the organisation that it becomes a problem. So, what is that proportion – 5% or 25% per annum? The answer is different for each organisation, and even for different staff levels within organisations. It is often better, therefore, to look at employee turnover in relation to industry averages. If your employee turnover rate is higher than the industry average you would benefit by considering steps to address this problem.

The link between employee development, employee satisfaction and employee retention has been established for some time, but some organisations miss a trick by not treating the whole issue of staff retention in a strategic manner. The first step is the development of an employee retention strategy that identifies the 'pinch points' for the organisation – the areas where the organisation regularly suffers from a high staff turnover and the particular concerns and problems of the targeted employee groups.

It is important to ask a number of questions in relation to the target groups, such as the following:

- Do these employees have the support they need to operate effectively?

- Are there opportunities to progress within the organisation?

- Are there opportunities to be trained to be able to take advantage of progression to higher-skilled, higher-paid work?

- What are the conditions for similar employees at competitors?

- Are you flexible in enabling employees to make their personal contribution in a way that fits in with the organisation and their own lives?

As an organisation, do you really understand the aspirations of your employees? Only when you have a clear understanding of the expectations and aspirations of your employees can you develop the strategies needed to meet some of these aspirations, eventually developing a workplace that is great to work in and with employees who see the organisation as good to work for.

A retention strategy should address such issues as support in the workplace, progression (as part of a plan), opportunities for development, remuneration, working time and flexible working.

Key to success

Although, clearly, a retention strategy will cover much more than development activities, it will be the integration of training and development within the retention strategy that will be the key to success. Training and development provides the means of supporting employees to operate effectively and enabling them to access the opportunities provided by the retention strategy. Levels of remuneration and flexible working will signal the right environment but it is through using training and development as a mechanism to demonstrate investment in employees on an ongoing basis that will turn organisational commitment in to reality.

For example, to move from an organisation that has inflexible work patterns and styles to one that encourages an array of diverse work modes is not straightforward. Many people will need the support of new skills to be able to take advantage of any change in work patterns – new skills such as work planning, time management and remote communication systems will be of crucial importance if real alternatives are to be offered.

The development of progression routes within an organisation is only viable if there are opportunities provided for individuals to gain the skills and experience needed to operate in a more senior post.

It could be wrong to think that merely offering training programmes to address these areas is sufficient. The success of an organisation's strategy will be judged ultimately by its success in *engaging individuals* in development activities, *not in merely having them available*. Many of these development activities, such as skill development for promotion, are often best met through activities such as coaching. Therefore, a precursor to implementing this aspect of a retention strategy may be to ensure all supervisors and managers have adequate coaching skills and support. The key to success will be how relevant and appropriate the development activity is and how accessible it is to employees.

Scott Watson

Increased employee retention will not be found through training alone but through a culture that values and responds to the needs of its workforce. People value time spent in an organisation that itself values their personal contribution. Moreover, people will stay with an organisation which has a culture that respects individuals for their diversity, their skills and their contribution, often at the expense of other employers who are prepared to offer higher inducements in salaries and other incentives. Employees understand the value of work-life balance and family-friendly flexibility that can help them to achieve this. Organisations that understand the value of such policies not only find it easier to retain employees but also to recruit and motivate them, and to reduce stress, sick leave and short-term absenteeism.

It could be misleading to assume that all employee retention issues can be addressed through fulfilling the explicit aspirations of employee groups. First, because such aspirations are rarely clear cut and explicit and, secondly, they are also linked to the perceptions that these employees have about the organisation. If I model the activities of employers who have high retention rates relative to competitors in their sector, I find that as well as highly-developed training and support structures for workers, there are excellent communication structures. Often, a significant level of public relations activity demonstrating community support and corporate responsibility complements this. It is important for organisations to provide reasons to their employees for being proud of their employer.

Future trends

The pressures on organisations to retain employees is likely to become more rather than less challenging if we look at future trends. Studies have pointed to a shift in the nature of how individuals view work and we can see that, in the future:

- Individuals will want to exercise greater choice over their lifestyle.

- Behaviours will be less conformist and more self-centred and indulgent.

- Individuals will be more mobile in all spheres of life, including work and employment.

- The traditional boundary between work and home will blur.

- Most people will be working but fewer will have jobs; the view of the job as the unit of production and the basis of careers will decline.

- Increasingly, people will work for themselves rather than someone else.

- Careers will continue to fragment, skill cycles will shorten and the need for re-skilling increase.

- A growing number of employees will think of their employment as temporary.

Holding onto good employees will become more and more of an issue as the perception of employment and work changes. However, the added value in using training and development as a tool for employee retention is clear, because by developing the environment that will retain employees as an organisation is also developing an environment that will increase attendance, company loyalty, skills, innovation and even production. The successful

Scott Watson

employers of the future will be keen competitors in the skills market. They will compete for the best recruits not in terms of purely financial rewards but by offering them the best working experience, one that offers security as well as progression and personal growth.

My Notes

Scott Watson

CHAPTER 14:
BEFORE YOU GO AND SPEND A PENNY...STOP!

With outsourcing becoming more popular, this chapter provides a practical guide to the often complex and time-consuming task of selecting the right provider.

Mounting pressures on decision makers to reduce employee head count and drive up key areas of performance quickly has raised the need for seeking help from external providers to deliver business critical projects. But with the vast number of providers in the market, the process of selecting a partner can be a headache in itself. And that's before your project has even started. How can you be sure that you are hiring the best supplier?

While there are no guarantees, the good news is that by using a practical, flexible approach you can maximise the potential of hiring the best possible support and minimise the risk of being stuck half way through a project feeling like a yacht cast adrift without direction.

So, what do you need to look for in a potential supplier or partner? After all, there are thousands of consultancies, service providers and training companies all screaming for your attention, some claiming to have 'the right mix between strategy and reality' or 'the latest big thing in enter-trainment'. But beyond the marketing blurb, how can you find whether they are credible? Do they have a proven track record in delivering excellent results for clients or are they just hoping that the latest buzzwords will be enough to attract you and secure a sale?

Do your groundwork

Before you go and spend a single penny...stop! Time spent in determining what you require, why you require it and the implications of outsourcing will all help you to select the right partner. Begin by asking yourself some key questions such as:

What is the rationale for outsourcing? Outsourcing may be seen as a way to save money, to obtain better quality services, to obtain expertise. Make sure you are clear about why the organisation is looking to outsource. Only by being clear about why you are engaging an outsource provider can you focus on the type of results you will need.

What is the risk involved? The consequence of a poorly chosen PC repair service provider (if you catch the damage early enough) might cost only a couple of PC's and annoyed internal users. But outsourcing your entire customer service support to the wrong provider could cost you a great deal in sales.

Once you have established a clear rationale for the outsourcing and have a clear understanding of the level of risk, you can start to determine the detailed specification. You can begin to describe what you will need from a potential partner, what you want the outsourcing organisation to provide, your budget and even shared accountability for the achievement of the results you need.

A good way of focusing on what you require is by determining how will performance be measured? For all outsourcing activity you will need to be specific about goals, deadlines and other deliverables, such as performance benchmarks. You need to think of not only the project deliverables but also the relationship with your organisation, e.g. how problems are to be addressed. If this is set up correctly at the outset the provider can be made responsible for tracking all the outputs and you will be responsible for spot-checks. The importance of not only collecting performance data but also making sure a pair of intelligent eyes scans it in time to address any shortcomings cannot be overemphasised.

Before you begin the selection process you need to be clear on:

1. ***The added value you expect external support to contribute***

2. ***Goals for the project and how success will be measured***

3. ***How you want the relationship to take shape.***

You can then begin to select a provider with a level of clarity that will underpin your selection process.

Think past the consultant's sales pitch

There are many ways that organisations choose outsourcing support. They include word-of-mouth referrals from a colleague or acquaintance, reputation within a certain industry sector, professional affiliations and the internet or even Yellow Pages.

But whoever you choose, how do you know that they have the capability, experience, expertise and attitude to work effectively with your organisation? Take the following steps and you will maximise your chances of selecting a capable and effective outsourcing partner. My goal is to encourage you to think past the consultant's sales pitch, which could be designed to secure a sale rather than answer your questions.

It is important to ask who will be involved in the day-to-day work on your project.

You may have heard statements from consultants such as *'Our people have worked in leadership or management positions in some of the world's leading companies'*, and maybe that is true. But while that may sound impressive, a good question to ask the consultant is *"But what did they deliver in terms of value and results?"* After all, this is your budget you are about to part with, and it is usually a lot more than spare change, so you deserve a precise answer. Don't be impressed by simply reading an impressive CV, dig deeper to ensure that you will get the best possible team to deliver your project. In selecting a provider you should ask yourself the following:

What are the credentials of the provider staff?

Qualifications aren't everything, but academic certification is one benchmark that tells you at what level of academic input the provider's staff has achieved. Whatever you use as a benchmark, insist upon knowing the basic qualifications of the individuals who will be working with your organisation and the nature and type of previous experience.

How consistent is the expertise level?

Bait and switch is one of the most annoying practices employed in the outsourcing and consultancy industry. Providers show up to the sales meeting with their top consultants, but when the contract has been secured, they deploy an inexperienced crew on your project. It is important to ask who will be involved in the day-to-day work on your project and ensure that you are comfortable with the resources allocated to your project.

Are reliable client testimonials available?

Not surprisingly, providers will give you only testimonials that are sure to check out well. However, do approach these referees but ask them questions that require a qualitative response. Don't just ask whether they were happy with the service; ask them to identify the top three areas where the service provider could improve to move up to the next level.

Does the provider look to solve your problems?

If you have a question about whether a particular service is within the contract, do your providers read the contract with an eagle eye to get the service included or push it out?

Are the deliverables realistic?

Beware of providers who promise the world. Do not trust those who gloss over what could be a complex project. Buying into professionals who are good at what they do, and who outline possible limitations and banana skins, is far better than falling for the sales pitch of a bubbly service provider representative who is eager to please and secure a sale.

How will the provider assist in-sourcing?

You do not want to be locked into a provider in such a way as to militate against switching providers or bringing the function in-house in the future. Answering these questions will help to identify potential partners who should be able to provide what you need. Once you have selected a provider it is imperative that you can agree a contract that assists in the smooth running of a genuine win-win client/provider relationship.

Getting the contract right

The contract is where all your assumptions about how the provider will work with you are made explicit. It is also the place where the provider's expectations of you are also made explicit. Enter into contract negotiations with a win-win proposition very much in mind. You want to achieve your outsourcing objective with your partner as smoothly and effectively as possible. The contract should allow the provider some flexibility, allow them to make a reasonable profit and enable them to do an excellent job for you.

Enter into contract negotiations with a win-win proposition

Nevertheless, from your perspective it is important that the contract takes account of performance. Whether the contract is time based or output based it should be broken down into small deliverables. Sometimes you will benefit more by purchasing these small deliverables individually within a contract, rather than committing to a large fee that covers a large project or period of time. However, economies of scale are likely to be a factor in larger contracts and therefore flexibility in delivery timetables could result in cost savings.

Do be careful about buying blocks of hourly or daily service, even though you are likely to receive a discount when buying in bulk. Do your homework before you commit to a contract where the provider collects fees based on a block of service time.

All contracts should address the issue of what happens if things go wrong. Unless counter-measures are built into a contract, there is a danger that service complaints will go nowhere quickly. The contract should explain what would be deemed as poor performance and how this is to be addressed. Be very clear. This will mean that you will have a responsibility for monitoring the work of your chosen provider. If you ignore your outsourcing vendor for some time, or until things are totally fouled up, you will be partly responsible.

Something to think about…

Set a clear context from the outset in the following areas:

- ✓ The timescales, budgets, priorities and resources available for the project.

- ✓ Set specific measures that allow you to monitor the success of the project and resolve any issues quickly and effectively.

- ✓ Insist on seeing client testimonials rather than just a CV – it is the best way to ensure that you will receive high quality support.

- ✓ Insist on the right to choose from a pool of consultants/trainers that you feel you can work well with and set the standards you need.

- ✓ Consider negotiating performance-related bonuses where the project fee quoted exceeds your budget but you want to appoint a certain supplier.

- ✓ Implement specific performance measures and keep everyone accountable for their achievement.

- ✓ Always start the procurement process with a win-win outcome in mind and invite the potential suppliers to do the same – open, honest communication adds so much value to the relationship even before you get started.

My Notes

Printed in the United Kingdom
by Lightning Source UK Ltd.
124523UK00003B/91-108/A

THE LIGHTS OF HOME